Scenic Walks
in Killarney

Jim Ryan is a civil engineer living in Cork. A regular walker in Ireland and abroad, he has a particular interest in geology and claims his spiritual home is on the Reeks of Kerry. His previous books include *Aconcagua – The Highest Trek in the World (2004)*, and *Carrauntoohil & MacGillycuddy's Reeks* (2006).

Parkavonear Castle

SCENIC WALKS IN KILLARNEY

A Walking Guide

Jim Ryan

The Collins Press

First published in 2012 by
The Collins Press
West Link Park
Doughcloyne
Wilton
Cork

British Library Cataloguing in Publication data

Ryan, Jim, 1946-
Scenic walks in Killarney : a walking guide.
1. Walking—Ireland—Killarney (Kerry)—Guidebooks.
2. Killarney (Kerry, Ireland)—Guidebooks.
I. Title
796.5'1'0941965-dc23

ISBN-13: 9781848891463

Design and typesetting by Fairways Design

Typeset in Avenir

Printed in the Czech Republic by Finidr

Cover photographs:
Front: the sixteenth-century Old Weir Bridge at 'The Meeting of the Waters', where the three lakes of Killarney meet; *back:* sunset at Ross Castle, Killarney National Park. (Photos courtesy Valerie O'Sullivan)

Contents

Acknowledgements

Sincere thanks are due to Kevin Tarrant and Eileen Daly for their reviews and useful comments, to Paudie O'Leary of the Killarney National Park, to Valerie O'Sullivan for her photos on the cover and pp 42–3 and 65, and to my wife and children who carried out trial runs of the walks.

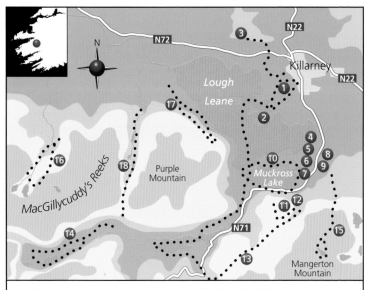

1 Town Centre to Ross Castle
2 Ross Island Circuit
3 Aghadoe to St Mary's Cathedral
4 Muckross Gardens, Arboretum and Traditional Farms
5 Arthur Young Nature Trail
6 Old Boathouse Nature Trail
7 Muckross Abbey Circuit
8 Blue Pool Nature Trail
9 Cloghereen Nature Trail
10 Circuit of Muckross Lake
11 Torc Waterfall
12 Torc Mountain
13 Lord Brandon's Cottage and Return by Boat
14 The Black Valley Circuit
15 Mangerton Mountain Circuit
16 Hag's Glen Circuit
17 Tomies Wood
18 The Gap of Dunloe

Overview Map

Walking Killarney

If you have purchased this guidebook it is probable that you have already been lured to Killarney. It may be pointless therefore to promote the sights that have attracted visitors for centuries. Now your focus will be to optimise your time here. It would be unfortunate for you to go away and discover that you missed some important features.

It is said that there is a walk for every day of the year in Killarney. The walks in this book include all of the important sights. They vary from short strolls that will only take an hour to those that require a day. Included in one of the walks is a boat trip, an essential item on any schedule in Killarney. When Queen Victoria visited Killarney in 1861 she came with a challenging schedule of walks, and, to the surprise of the locals, adhered to it. Her schedule had a mixture of nature trails, woodland and even mountain walks.

The prerequisites for a walk should be a good balance of physical exercise, vista and awareness of the flora and fauna. A basic appreciation of the history and folklore is a vital ingredient that can enhance the experience.

There are walks here for the energetic and for those restricted to the flat. The times suggested for each walk are for guidance and assume a relatively leisurely pace, with time to savour, time to look at nature. Walkers are asked to adhere to the custom of 'leave no trace', removing all their rubbish and not interfering with nature in any way. Do not pick flowers or take cuttings. Make sure that you are prepared, with a fully charged mobile phone for emergencies, and that someone is aware of your route and timetable.

If you have the energy to tackle more strenuous walks or you would like to read more about the high mountains then you might consider *Carrauntoohil and MacGillycuddy's Reeks* by the same author and publisher.

WALK 1
TOWN CENTRE TO ROSS CASTLE

LENGTH: 5 km.
DURATION: 2 hours, excluding exploration of the castle.
DIFFICULTY: Easy, flat, on paved paths.
INTEREST: Historic castle, lake views, woodland walk.
START/FINISH: Town centre.
OPTIONS: This walk may be combined with the Ross Island walk. There is a cafe at the castle.

Ross Castle

For any visitor to Killarney a visit to Ross Castle should be a high priority. The town of Killarney was built because of the castle at Ross so that, throughout history, activities at the castle dictated what transpired in the town. The castle is open to the public for most of the year.

Start

We walk from the town centre out the Muckross Road, in the direction of Kenmare. The first road on the right is Ross Road. This leads directly to the castle.

Outward Journey

Before we reach Ross Road, the gates on our right and the demesne walls that we pass surrounded the estate of the Browne family of Killarney House. Although the Brownes, of whom many had the Christian name of Valentine, were Catholics,

Ross Castle

Ross Castle is a most important building in the Killarney area. Indeed, Ross Castle was there before the town, and the town was built up around the castle. Its history is chequered with disputes over ownership, legal quarrels over title, sieges and battles for control of it and tales of extraordinary men who came to it.

The main fortified town house was built by O'Donoghue Mór, the local Irish chieftain, in the early fifteenth century. He used it as his residence and headquarters, collecting tithes on butter and oatmeal production. O'Donoghue Mór lost the castle to the crown when he was found guilty of treason after a rebellion in 1583. The families of Browne and McCarthy fought legal disputes over its ownership during the early seventeenth century.

Perhaps the most famous story about the castle is that of 1652 when Lord Muskerry, uncle of the young owner, Valentine Browne, and leader of the Catholic Confederate army, took it over in defiance of the Parliament forces. Ross Castle was the last stronghold in Ireland to hold out in the rebellion of 1641–52. Parliament had dispatched General Ludlow to capture it. He laid siege to the castle, intending to starve those inside (they numbered 5,000). However, there was a prophecy about the castle which suggested *that it should never be taken until a ship should swim upon the lake*. Ludlow had a ship prefabricated in Kinsale and transported to Kerry where carpenters assembled it and floated it out onto Lough Leane. The sight of the ship on the lake had a profound effect on the outcome of the altercation. Whether Muskerry considered his flank to be vulnerable from the lakeside or whether he believed the prophecy, we shall never know, but, in any event, he capitulated and surrendered.

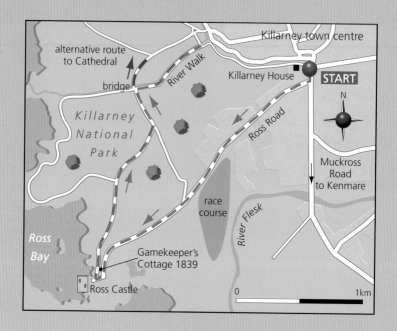

Killarney town centre

alternative route
to Cathedral

Killarney House

START

bridge

River Walk

N

Killarney

Ross Road

National

Park

Muckross
Road
to Kenmare

race
course

River Flesk

Ross
Bay

Gamekeeper's
Cottage 1839

Ross Castle

0   1km

Ross Castle

they were very influential and were honoured in 1861 by the visit of Queen Victoria. The Brownes had built a magnificent house near Knockreer in 1872, but it was destroyed by fire in 1913 and was not rebuilt. The current Killarney House is a rather mundane structure, developed by converting former stables.

Halfway along Ross Road we are out of the town and into the country. On our right we see a very old house, with the year it was built, 1839, over the doorway. It is just across the road from the 'wishing well'. The old house is the former gamekeeper's cottage.

As we proceed huge lime trees line the road on our right all the way to the castle car park. We cross a wooden bridge and enter the castle through a gate on the right.

It is interesting first to take a walk around the castle, to experience its scale. We notice that it is solidly founded on limestone rock. Situated in a sheltered bay its location is strategic, enabling those who commanded the castle to control the island also.

Return

Our return to the town is through the Killarney National Park. After crossing the wooden bridge we veer left away from Ross Road and into the mature woodland. We walk through a forest of young oaks in wet bog land. These oaks have been rejuvenated in recent times as the rhododendrons that engulfed them were cut and cleared. We can still see piles of cut rhododendrons, and we will notice that some seedlings managed to survive the 'foreigner cleansing'.

Following the signs for Knockreer House we come to a path junction where we have the choice of going right, returning to town along the bank of the river, or going through the open field of the national park. If we choose the latter we will emerge at the park gate across the road from St Mary's Cathedral, passing the thatched Deenagh Lodge on the way.

Deenagh Lodge

Rhododendrons

Clearance of the Rhododendron

Rhododendron was introduced into Killarney in the nineteenth century. It gradually migrated through the parkland, its tentacles spreading out and engulfing native species. In the wet Irish climate it has flourished and spread much more than in the countries it is native to (such as Spain, Portugal, Turkey and countries in Asia). Its shiny leaves block out the light to the undergrowth and its flowers have thousands of seeds. Through years of painstaking work the parkland forestry managed to cut much of it out. Assistance was provided by volunteers, some of them from overseas, who came to Killarney during the summer to hack down the invader. It continues to be a nuisance in the area and can be seen spreading through areas such as the Gap of Dunloe. The Killarney National Park's long-term goal is to eradicate it fully, but they recognise the enormous task still ahead of them. On the Torc Waterfall walk we will see the most extensive area of rhododendron.

WALK 2
ROSS ISLAND CIRCUIT

LENGTH:	4.5 km.
DURATION:	2 hours.
DIFFICULTY:	Relatively easy, on paved paths.
INTEREST:	Largest trees in Killarney, old copper mines, vantage points for views over the lake. Red squirrels. Possibility of spotting eagles.
START/FINISH:	Ross Castle.
OPTIONS:	This walk may be combined with the walk to Ross Castle. The length of the walk may be reduced to 2.5 km by not going out to Library Point.
There is a cafe at the castle.

Silver Fir

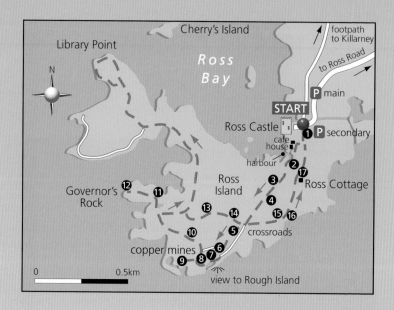

The circuit is a figure of eight, with an offshoot in the middle. We will follow limestone markers all the way. On the walk we will see some of the finest specimens of trees in the country. We will see Bronze Age mines and read information notices about their workings. If we have binoculars, we can look out for eagles over the lake.

Start

As we approach Ross Castle from the car park there is a sign to the left for the island walk. However, our walk does not initially follow the main path. A few metres beyond the start of the main path we take the first narrow path to the right that leads to a small harbour.

1. We must find the limestone marker adjacent to Ross Castle so we are familiar with the markers en route. Beside it there is a plaque saying 'Ross Island Mining Trail'.

2. The marker is at a small harbour used for mooring boats. Our route is along the edge of the harbour, then leaving the harbour to go into the woods. In springtime the woods will be filled with bluebells and there will be the distinctive scent of wild garlic. Between here and the next marker we also see ash, birch and yew clinging to the bare rock.

3. This marker is on our left. It is before a cave in the limestone. We are in an area of wet woodland that floods when the lake level is high. Alder trees thrive in these swampy conditions.

The Bronze Age in Britain began in Killarney

Mining began in Killarney over 4,000 years ago. Copper from Ross Island was the first metal ever cast in these islands. Ross Island copper was exported to Britain from 2,500 BC and continued, intermittently, right up to 1912. Although the predominant metal mined was copper, there was also silver, lead and zinc. At the height of production the mines employed hundreds of men; 200 tons of copper a year were exported and 400 tons of Welsh coal were required annually to keep the mines going.

In order to understand why there was ever mining in this area of Ireland we must look to geology. There is an enormous geological fault in the bedrock on a line from Muckross to Millstreet, and this passes close to Ross Island and Muckross Lake. Along this fault the bedrock to the south is some 3,000 metres higher than that to the north. The formation of the fault was accompanied by enormous heat. The dispersed metals in the rock melted and were redeposited in concentrated lodes and veins.

4. Close to the previous marker we can see that the limestone is horizontally bedded. This is Carboniferous Limestone, approximately 300 million years old. The limestone contains the fossilised remains of sea creatures and plants, all cemented together. The acidic soils and vegetation that surround the high ground around Killarney produces a mildly acidic run-off that, over geological time, dissolves the limestone.

5. We walk on through the wood to arrive at a crossroad. This is our cross-over on our return. The path to the left takes us back to Ross Castle, the next on our left will take us down to the shore of the lake. We will take the next path on the left, following the sign for the mining trail. At the marker there is a quarry on our right. Dating to the eighteenth and nineteenth centuries, the quarry produced stone for building purposes, mainly for the mines.

6. We are now overlooking the Blue Hole. The colour of the water in the hole is due to the composition of the minerals in the rock.

7. The marker overlooks an ancient coffer dam. The pond was used as a pumping pit to keep the mines free of water. Around the pond sea pinks are abundant in the early summer. Looking out into the lake the nearest island to us, directly south, is Rough Island and this is the nearest vantage point to it. Occasionally eagles may be seen around the island because this is where culled deer carcasses are left for the eagles to feed on.

8. This is the site of the industrial mine. In contrast to the open-mine system, shafts were sunk and tunnels made to extract the ore. Fifty such shafts have been identified on Ross Island. It is worth a diversion here to wander down to the lakeshore where, during dry periods, we will see how the lake water

Sea pinks amongst pine roots

has eroded the soil, exposing the roots of the Scots pines. Flowers such as sea pinks and sea campions flourish among the exposed roots.

9. We take a short spur off the trail to reach the Bronze Age mine. It has been dated, through archaeological excavations, to 2300–2100 BC. We must retrace our steps back to the path to turn left. At the next crossroads we turn left in the direction of Governor's Rock and Library Point. However, before doing so we make a small diversion to the right, and after 40 metres we can look down into the depths of an open-cast mine.

10. En route to Governor's Rock the marker is on our left and there is a yew tree on either side of the track, each quite different in structure. Yew wood was used for making fine furniture of rich colour and interesting grain. It was also used for the making of longbows.

11. As we approach Governor's Rock a masonry stile is in our path. This was part of a fence on the island during a period when feral goats were a problem.

12. There is a short climb up the limestone rock to a guard rail on Governor's Rock. Looking directly out into Lough Leane we have Torc Mountain on our left and Purple Mountain on our right. Between the two is the channel that connects Lough Leane to Muckross Lake at Brickeen Bridge and Dinish Island. Below the guard rail on the left is an arbutus tree. We also note that little oaks have managed to cling to the rock. Looking away from the lake view there is a small oak behind us that looks almost like a bonsai.

Returning from Governor's Rock to the path we turn left. At the next crossroads we will go left again, out to Library Point. There are no markers on this part of the walk. The path now undulates out along the peninsula, with oak and beech competing for dominance. As we approach Library Point the path divides, providing a circuit. The views from Library Point are towards the northern side of the lake. The island on the left is Innisfallen where there is an old monastery, and the small island between it and the mainland is known as O'Donoghue's Prison.

Viewed from the lake the rocks at Library Point, also known as O'Donoghue's Library, appear to be stacked like books.

The Return

Returning to the crossroads we turn left and, after a short walk, we come back to the markers.

Monterey pine

13. We have reached the area of giant Monterey pines. There are three here and another further along on our right. These specimens have an age of over 150 years. They have a faster growth rate here than they do in their native California. Also in this area there is a large Western Red Cedar and a Portuguese Laurel.

14. The marker is on the left before we reach the main crossroads. There is a beech forest surrounding the Monterey pines in this location. There is one large beech that has lost two of its branches, providing holes for birds to nest.

15. Marker 15 is near where there is a large boulder sitting loosely on the rock. This is an 'erratic', a sandstone boulder, older than the limestone it sits on, deposited on it during the Ice Age. We are told that the ice was up to a kilometre thick. The sandstone of the erratic tells us that the route of the ice was from the south where the sandstone is, towards the north, which is underlain by limestone.

16. On the left of the path we encounter the largest silver fir tree in Killarney. It has enormous branches leaning towards the lake. Seventy metres further along we see a large copper beech, whose leaves are a mild, autumn shade. Out in the lake we can see a range of islands; from the left they are Swallow Island, Crow Island, Cow Island and Rough Island. Crow Island was the site of a copper mine during the early nineteenth century.

17. The ruins of Ross Cottage. This was a thatched cottage built in the *orné* style, some would say an imitation of vernacular homesteads. It is said that the poet Percy Shelley stayed in this cottage in 1812 where he completed his epic poem *Queen Mab*.

> *Though storms may break the primrose on its stalk,*
> *Though frosts may blight the freshness of its bloom,*
> *Yet spring's awakening breath will woo the earth*
> *To feed with kindliest dews its favourite flower,*
> *That blooms in mossy bank and darksome glens,*
> *Lighting the greenwood with its sunny smile.*

WALK 3
AGHADOE TO ST MARY'S CATHEDRAL

LENGTH:	4.5 km.
DURATION:	1½ to 2 hours.
DIFFICULTY:	Easy. On roads and paved paths. Downhill or on the flat.
INTEREST:	Stunning views over Killarney. Walk through pastures of the National Park where we may see deer. Experience Pugin's great cathedral.
START/FINISH:	Start at the Aghadoe Heights Hotel. Finish in the town.
OPTIONS:	The gardens of Knockreer House, which is on our route, may be visited.

View from Aghadoe over the town towards the mountains

Start

For this walk we will take a taxi to the Aghadoe Heights Hotel. From there we will be walking downhill all the way back to town. In front of the hotel there is a flat field with a seat. From this magnificent vantage point we can see over the town of Killarney. Starting on our right the first range of mountains is the MacGillycuddy's Reeks, with Carrauntoohil, the highest mountain in Ireland, on the left side of this cluster. The slope away from Carrauntoohil leads to the col of the Devil's Ladder. From the col the land rises up to the cluster of the Eastern Reeks. The third cluster includes the mountains of Purple and Tomies, whilst around to our left we finally come to Mangerton.

Red Deer And Sika Deer

Red deer

Sika deer

There are two distinct species of deer in the national park, the indigenous red deer who have been here for thousands of years, and the grey sika deer who were introduced in 1865 (for hunting). The numbers for both are roughly similar at between 600 and 800. Since they have no natural predators, annual culling is necessary in the management of the park, and this can be over 100 in any year. The red deer will be seen more on the open parklands. Sika deer are very shy; they like the shelter afforded by the forest, and in particular the shelter of rhododendrons.

Outward Journey

Walking in front of the hotel we take the narrow road on our right before a ruined church and a graveyard. The church was formerly the cathedral of Aghadoe. The monastic settlement of Aghadoe is very old, and is believed to have been founded in the tenth century. After a few metres on our right we reach Parkavonear Castle. This round tower is a thirteenth-century Norman keep, the inner fortress of a squared enclosure that had earthen banks forming the outer perimeter. The keep has been referred to in the area as the 'bishop's chair' or the 'pulpit', probably because of its proximity to the cathedral.

The road from Parkavonear Castle is initially quite steep, but then flattens as it passes behind the golf course. This is **Bóthirín na Marbh** (Boreen na Marv), or 'the lane of the dead'. It was an old funeral route possibly linking Aghadoe to the lakeshore and the Innisfallen monastery. On the steep descent we enjoy more fine views of the town below and the mountains in the background. There are very fine houses on this road, most especially one that has boulders forming its boundary. We emerge from the narrow road alongside horse stables. Here

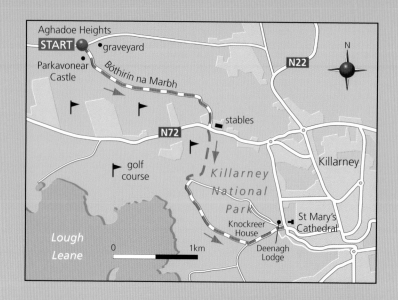

Aghadoe Heights
START
graveyard
Parkavonear
Castle
Bóthirín na Marbh
N22
N
N72
stables
Killarney
golf
course
Killarney
National
Park
Knockreer
House
St Mary's
Cathedral
Lough
Leane
0   1km
Deenagh
Lodge

Aghadoe

Parkavonear Castle

we must pause and carefully cross the main road going direct into the Killarney National Park. We follow the path that runs parallel to the bridle path, rising up to give us a fine view down to the lake. With the golf course on our right we come to a gate into the park. We take the narrow stone path to the right that takes us to a paved path that is known as 'The Circular Walk' and we will follow it in an anticlockwise direction. Our walk passes through some woodland, but is mostly in open parkland. If we look over into the woods there is every likelihood of spotting deer.

Return

The circular walk takes us in the direction of Knockreer House. This building is on a plateau above the park and we skirt under its embankment. As we rise up towards the park gate, ahead of us is the imposing spire of St Mary's Cathedral.

The path passes the picturesque thatched Deenagh Lodge. It was the gatehouse to the Kenmare Estate. We can imagine the privileged hunters outside

Stained glass detail, St Mary's Cathedral

What the Jarvey said to the Yank

A jarvey was taking a group of Americans out from the town to the Gap of Dunloe. One of the party, a loud-mouthed fellow, sat up beside the jarvey. On the way he was blowing about how better things were in the States, how faster things got done, etc. The jarvey was getting fed up with him. The Yank told about how builders in the States could prefabricate parts of the structure off site, so that the construction period was very short. The jarvey took a different route back into town, one that went past the Cathedral. 'That's a fine looking building,' said the yank. 'And it looks new, as well.'

'God, sir, I don't know where it came out of,' said the jarvey, 'for it wasn't there this morning.' He was seen to wink at those in the back of the carriage.

it, with their guns and dogs, sipping port, whilst their helpers and threshers anxiously waited for the day's hunt to begin. During the summer the Lodge is open as a tea room.

Across the road from the gates of the National Park is St Mary's Cathedral. This fine structure was designed by the renowned architect Augustus Pugin. Construction began in 1842, but was abandoned during the years of the Great Famine (1845–49) when the partially constructed building was used to house famine victims. Pugin was never to see the completed work. The stained glass windows are of exceptional quality. To the right of the main altar we see the coat of arms of the Browne family on the tiled floor and at the base of the centre lancets of the stained glass rear window, a testament to the sponsorship that the family gave in the construction of the cathedral.

MUCKROSS GARDENS, ARBORETUM AND TRADITIONAL FARMS

LENGTH:	Gardens walk 1.5 km, farms another 1.5 km
DURATION:	Half a day to a day.
DIFFICULTY:	Relatively flat.
INTEREST:	Wonderful specimen trees, shrubs and flowers, rural folkways and bygone traditions.
START/FINISH:	Muckross House.
OPTIONS:	The walk can be split into the two parts: gardens and farms. A visit to Muckross House can be added. There is a restaurant and a souvenir shop at Muckross House.

Sunken Garden

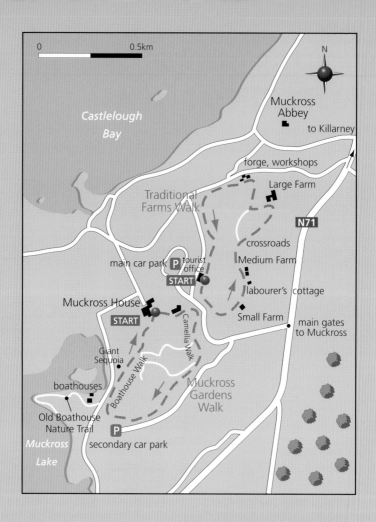

The acquisition of Muckross by the Irish State, its preservation and enhancement, places it to the forefront of national peoples' facilities. With Muckross as the fulcrum we have the most complete choice of activity, from a historic tour of the great house, a stroll around the gardens and arboretum, to adventures into lakes and woodland. Just as Killarney is a 'must' for any visitor to Ireland, so too is Muckross a 'must' for the Killarney visitor. But it is not simply tourists who frequent the place. By far the majority of those who come to Muckross are from the locality, enjoying this great national treasure.

Our walk is set out so that we experience the important garden, arboretum and farm features whilst simultaneously availing of a few hours' healthy exercise. In the gardens we will walk in a clockwise direction and reverse this direction to view the farms. The farms are not open all the time, generally confined to the afternoons, and only at weekends in the early summer and autumn, so it is wise to walk the gardens in the morning.

Muckross – Built to Attract Royalty

The Herberts of Muckross came to Ireland in the early seventeenth century as part of an Elizabethan plantation. They were a very influential family, not just in Ireland. Their power reached its zenith with Henry William Herbert (1815–66) who was appointed chief secretary of Ireland. Henry built Muckross in 1838 in the Scottish Baronial style, which was most fashionable at the time, Balmoral Castle being an important example. Not only did Henry employ a prominent Scottish architect, he also brought over to Ireland Scottish craftsmen to construct the house. It is said that Henry's motive in the construction of the house was to entice the King (or Queen) of England to visit. No expense was spared on the house, the estate and the surrounding lands. Following Queen Victoria's visit in 1861 it was the expectation that Henry would be favoured with a knighthood, a title that did not materialise. Within five years of the queen's visit Henry was dead, felled by the same ailment – apoplexy – that killed his father. Within twenty years crippling debts at Muckross resulted in the estate having to be sold, and no Herberts have lived there since.

Start

We make our way to the cafeteria at the side of Muckross House from where we can look out through the rear glazing at our route. Directly in front of us are flowerbeds with a border of box hedging. Beyond them and the lawns there is a dome-shaped glazed greenhouse. This is the **conservatory** and we will pass to the right of it. Our route will be to go clockwise, returning back to the cafeteria. We can exit the cafeteria between it and the old greenhouse.

The Gardens and Arboretum

The **conservatory** once housed grapevines and other exotic fruit trees for the use of the Herberts. Now it is a nursery. Along the gravel path the strawberry-shaped bushes that define the corners of the lawns are yew trees. The mountain above the conservatory is Mangerton, and to the right is Torc Mountain. Before the gate we turn to our right. We pass a *Nothofagus dombeyi* tree. Sometimes known as the 'southern beech' this tree is native to the foothills of the Andes in

Chile. If we look to our right, beyond the lawn to the corner of the house, we are afforded a fine view of the great oak of Muckross.

We follow the sign for the arboretum and pass through a pedestrian gate in the fence. Directly ahead of us there is a large pine tree with the label *Pinus Radiata* on it. This is a Monterey pine. If we examine the fallen needles from it on the ground we see that they have three stems. Scots pines, by contrast, have only two stems. We carry on straight, with the pine on our right, up to the wall and turn right along the **Camellia Walk**. The various camellias are labelled: Red Moon, Spring Triumph, Glacier, etc. This part of the walk takes us past some fine oaks and yews. We take a right at the next junction (beyond the wall), keeping the fence on our left and avoiding paths into the Old Woodland on our right.

Just beyond a small cave in the limestone there is a large multi-stemmed ash tree. Across the path from it we notice the distinctive brown bark of myrtle trees. Further on we go left, following the signs for **Conifer & Birch Collections**. Very shortly we look out for the wooden sculpture by Gerard Cox, erected in 1989, entitled **'The Oak Spirit'**. It is partly hidden by a cypress. Further along the path we can see the gazebo through the trees. We are now in the area known as **The Italian Collection**. There are gum trees here and weeping birches. We follow the path with the fence now on our right.

As we approach the car park we turn to our right and go through the fence following the sign for boat trips. Below us is the busy main path that passes the shores of the lake, but we will take the first path before this, turning to our right. Before leaving the path junction we may like to make a short detour down towards the boathouse where there is a mighty Monterey Cypress. The tree is over 400 years old.

Following the path that runs above and parallel to the main path we are on the **Boathouse Walk**. We look out for the large tree on our left. It is a **Giant Redwood**, *Sequoiadendron giganteum*, all the way from the slopes of the Sierra Nevada in California. This tree will eventually outgrow all others in the gardens in size, height and age. At the next junction we turn right where there is a sign prohibiting football and cycling. We ascend, then descend to the area of **tree ferns**. These are best seen in late summer or in the autumn.

At the next junction we go to our left into the **Stream Garden**, and we follow the stream to reach the **hydrangea border**. The predominant colour of the flowers is blue, since the soil is relatively acidic. This takes us to the southern side of the main house. Our direction now is away from the lake and towards the main house. There is a fine **heather border** here as we pass beside the house and the Monterey pine to reach the **Sunken Garden** on our left and the **Rock Garden** on our right. Let us see if we can find the Chilean holly with its drooping flowers.

The Traditional Farms

To access the traditional farms we must go to the east of the car park into the cottage building that has the 'information' sign over the door. There is a small charge to visit the farms, and entrants are required to view them in an anticlockwise direction. At the various farms we will meet well-versed farming people who will tell us about the old ways and allow us to sample some of their products.

The first building we come to is a **small-sized farm**, typical of a farmer with 20 acres. This building would have been thatched. It has a henhouse at one end and a stable at the other. Inside we see a settle, which doubled as a bed for the children at night and a press by day. There is a fine dresser and all of the cooking is carried out on an open-hearth fire. Across the road in the field we can see the black cattle for which this area of Kerry is renowned.

Up the hill there is a slated, two-storey **labourer's cottage**. It has a very confined interior and the sleeping quarters upstairs have limited headroom. We move from there to a **medium-sized farm**. The main house is thatched. Removed from it at the rear is a stable. The farmer would have had a holding of 40 to 50 acres.

En route to the **large farm** we pass a crossroads, which would have been a traditional meeting place frequented by musicians who would play for the locals to dance to. The large farm is an expansive area with a haggard (high shed for storing hay) at one end. Often between the main house and the stables the yard might be referred to as a 'street'. This farm would typically have had a 100-acre holding.

To complete our tour we can call to look at the **small farm animals**, the **carpenter's workshop**, the **harness maker's workshop** and finally the **blacksmith's forge**.

Camellia   *Large farm yard*

WALK 5
THE ARTHUR YOUNG NATURE TRAIL

LENGTH:	5 km (figure of eight).
DURATION:	2 to 3 hours.
DIFFICULTY:	Some parts on inclined narrow paths over the rock. Some sections on soft ground.
INTEREST:	Walk in woodland and along the lakeshore, with detailed notes on the plants, geology and scenery.
START/FINISH:	Muckross House.
OPTIONS:	This walk can be curtailed at a number of points. There is good restaurant at Muckross House.

Colleen Bawn Rock

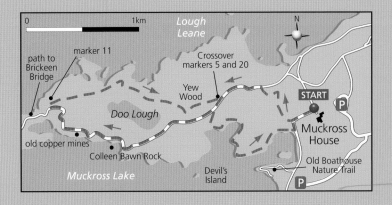

Arthur Young was an eighteenth-century English agriculturist who wrote discourses on landscapes and farming. He came to Ireland in 1776 and spent some time in Muckross, the guest of the estate owner at the time, Thomas Herbert. He went on this walk and wrote notes on what he encountered. The walk is set out with limestone markers that correspond with Young's notes. The markers occasionally become displaced or overgrown. If we cannot locate some it will not take from our enjoyment of the walk and we can proceed to the next one. As we walk the markers are all on the left-hand side of the path. Young's notes are set out in our walk description in *italics*.

Start

With the main portico of Muckross House at our back we walk towards the main approach avenue and take the first path on our left. We walk along this straight path for approximately 60 metres. On our right, over grassy ground we see a stone plaque beside a steel pedestrian gate.

Outward Journey

1. *Mr. Herbert has reclaimed 140 acres that were covered in rocks, stones, brambles and furze. He set fire to those areas he could not cut down and grub up. Some of the stones that he attacked were five to six feet square; the large ones were burst to pieces by kindling fires upon them, being brown sandstones, others were drawn off by bullocks, to some of which 30 were harnessed.* It is believed that the brown sandstones that Young referred to must have been what are geologically referred to as 'erratics', boulders that were transported by the ice age glacier and left behind when the glacier retreated about 13,000 years ago. We will see some of these on the walk. We pass three giant oaks and leave the open grassland via another pedestrian gate.

23

Arthur Young plaque   *Devil's-bit scabious*

2. Just before we reach this marker we see the yew trees growing on the mound of bare limestone that Herbert found it impossible to move. We notice the rhododendrons on our right that have survived the recent great clearance and have begun to regenerate. Immediately above the limestone marker stone there is a hart's-tongue fern, very common in the park.

3. Before we reach this marker we pass a giant Monterey pine. If we search the ground we should find some the needles of this tree. Through the trees ahead we see the waters of Lough Leane. The low land to our right, populated by alder trees, was once part of that lake, but sediment has formed to allow a bog to develop. The alders, which love waterlogged soil, have broad, flat end leaves and they are the only deciduous tree to bear cones.

4. The path now emerges onto the main, paved path. We will stay on this path out over the headland until we begin our return journey. *'Mr. Herbert's new road is carried in so judicious a manner through a variety of ground that nothing can be more pleasing; it passes through a remarkable scene of rocks which are covered with woods.'* As we round a bend in the path there is a narrow path on our right that climbs up to a small cave in the limestone. We pass the sign and path for Reenadinna Yew Wood that is on our right (we will emerge out here on the return journey).

5. Ignore the arrow for marker 20 and continue on the main path through a set of pillars. We are now at Pillar Hill. At the bottom of Pillar Hill the swampland supports the aromatic shrub, bog myrtle.

6. This marker is 50 metres beyond a sharp left-hand bend. It is several metres away from the road on our left. The swampy land and lake on our right is Doo Lough and it is on the boundary of the sandstone and the limestone. The swamp here is 7 metres in depth. Boreholes sunk through it have been radiocarbon dated providing us with some interesting insights into the history of the area. The deepest layers of the bog are 12,000 years old and were deposited following the last ice age in Ireland; the Killarney woodlands

became established 1,800 years ago. In this boggy land the devil's-bit scabious flourishes in the late summer.

7. A beach at the lakeshore provides a pleasant place for us to stop. Looking out across the lake we see the outline of Torc Mountain. *Full in front Turk Mountain rises with the proudest outline, in that abrupt magnificence which fills up the whole space before one, and closes the scene.* We are looking at the steepest side of Torc – on the south side its gradient is gentler. This is because we are looking directly at the great fault in the land. The top of Torc Mountain is many millions of years older than the rock we are standing on. The Muckross/Millstreet fault occurred 290 million years ago when the then continent of Africa collided with Europe resulting in enormous upheaval and shearing of the land. It pushed up the land on the south of the fault by 3,000 metres.

8. From *thence to the marble quarry which Mr. Herbert is working.* Unfortunately the marble quarry is overgrown and not possible to examine. In 1770 slabs of this fine marble was used as flags for a house for the Herberts at Muckross.

9. **Colleen Bawn Rock**. (This is the image depicted above at the introduction to this walk) There is another beach on the lakeshore and from it there is a narrow causeway that leads to the Colleen Bawn Rock ('the rock of the white girl'). Legend has it that the white girl, suffering from a broken heart because she was rejected by the son of the local lord, died when she threw herself off the rock.

10. We have now reached the area of the old copper mines of Muckross. On our right we have passed the ruin of a fine circular structure, and we now come to the powder magazine building. Across the road from the powder magazine is another ruin, thought to have been the residence of the superintendent of the mines. '*The road leads to a place where copper mines were worked; many shafts appear; as much ore was raised as sold twenty-five thousand pounds.*'

11. *To the left is a small bay, hemmed in by a neck of land in front.* There is a seat overlooking the bay and a boulder that affords us a better view. However, it is worth the trouble to slip through the trees down to the water's edge. Camillan Point is the headland that encloses the bay. This is a haunt for otters, but we are only likely to see them early in the morning or late in the evening. Looking out across the lake we can see the outline of the Eagles' Nest. Golden eagles soared over this area until the beginning of the twentieth century when they died out. In taking tourists for boat rides around the lakes it was the practice to fire a shot in the air to disturb the eagles. A few years ago eagles were successfully brought back to Kerry and it is hoped that soon we will have breeding pairs in the vicinity. As we come back onto the path we notice that the mighty oaks are the species sessile oak.

Return

When we reach the next junction in the path we will turn to the right for the return journey. En route from marker 11 we may notice a foreign tree on our right. It is the unmistakeable Chilean Pine, or monkey puzzle tree. There is an arrow marker that directs us to the left at the road junction. We may make a detour off our route to walk the 500 metres beyond it along the path to Brickeen Bridge where there are fine views.

12. The return path is newly surfaced. It cuts through woodland that has been cleared of rhododendron. Indeed, the rhododendron had completely engulfed the path itself.

13. Our route is through mature woodland with many trees covered in lichens. The ground cover includes wood sorrel (a tall plant) and tormentil (yellow-flowering leaves).

14. The marker is beside a mighty oak. *Caught a very agreeable view of Ash Island. Seen through an opening, enclosed on both sides by woods.* If we move to the right of the oak over beside the beech tree we get a better view of what Young is referring to. Ash Island is a small island in the distance. On the ground between the oak and the beech we notice the grass-like plant, woodrush.

15. The fenced area is intended to show how the woodland behaves in the absence of grazing animals, principally the sika deer. This Asian species was introduced to Killarney in 1865.

16. We skirt along the fence between the grass field and the wood, moving from oaks to yews. Out in the meadow in early summer wild flowers mingle amongst the grasses.

17. The marker is inside the fence. We see the floor of the yew forest coated in rich moss with occasional ferns spreading their arms.

18. The National Park has fenced many areas to keep out the deer and to protect the yew saplings. Holly is becoming established under the yews.

19. Beyond this marker there is an area where some specimen trees have been planted. They include a copper beech, Monterey pine, silver fir, American scarlet oak and American black oak.

20. We emerge again onto the main path we came out on. However, instead of going back to the left we double back to our right until we again meet marker 5 and follow the arrow for marker 20. The path now is narrower and undulating, over Carboniferous Limestone rock. This marker is on the ground on our left. Behind it there is a profusion of hard ferns. Back behind the marker, on the bank of the rock are hart's-tongue ferns. The latter thrives on a lime-rich base in contrast to the hard fern which likes the acid-rich soil.

21. Climbing two sets of steps we arrive at an area where there is a good view of the lake. Around us are arbutus trees, with their flaky barks. They are often referred to as *strawberry trees*, because their fruit is not unlike a strawberry, but is extremely bitter.

22. The marker is on our right where cotoneaster is spreading over the limestone. This particular species of shrub was transported from eastern Asia and planted here. It will only grow out in the open and does not like shady areas.

23. On our route to this marker, which is on our right in a stone plinth that we can rest on, we will pass a fine example of an erratic. It is a boulder of Old Red Sandstone that has been moved by a glacier during the last ice age and deposited here on top of the limestone.

24. Only 20 metres further on we get a view out over the lake where we can see Devil's Island.

25. We descend, stepping out of Carboniferous Limestone back into Old Red

Moss-covered ground in the yew forest   *Arthur Young Trail*

Sandstone, and immediately notice how the vegetation changes. If we are lucky to be here in late April there will be bluebells on the ground. There is a mighty Monterey pine here. As we proceed our path is always to follow close to the lakeshore, ignoring other paths to our left.

26. As we walk along this stretch we can look down at the lakeshore and see the tall Scots pines that line the shore. It is thought that these trees germinated from seeds that floated from the pine plantation across the lake in Torc some eighty years ago.

27. Beyond a multi-stemmed oak we can pause at this marker. If we peer through the trees we can see on the far side of the lake how the acidic waters have eroded the limestone.

28. *The view of the promontory of Dundag closes this part of the lake and is indeed singularly beautiful. It is a large rock which shoots out far into the water, of a height sufficient to be interesting, in full relief, fringed with a scanty vegetation.*

29. After we have descended a set of steps we are treated to a vista with Muckross House in the background and the lake in our foreground. This was not the house that Arthur Young stayed in when he visited, for this house was built only in 1843, sixty-seven years after his visit.

30. The final marker on our walk is on the path that passes between a limestone reef on our left and the lakeshore lapping the side of the walk on our right. From where we stand we can see gorse, then the white and pink flowers of valerian. There are laurel, cotoneaster and some small arbutus trees, all of them clinging to the rock where there is very little soil. Finally at the top we see dwarf yews.

WALK 6
THE OLD BOATHOUSE NATURE TRAIL

LENGTH:	1 km (circuit).
DURATION:	One hour.
DIFFICULTY:	Short, easy walk. One set of steps to descend, otherwise virtually flat, on gravel paths.
INTEREST:	Through a yew wood and arbutus grove, good lake views, interesting vegetation.
START/FINISH:	Muckross House.
OPTIONS:	The walk can be combined with a diversion over to Torc Waterfall, or with exploring Muckross House and its arboretum.

The nineteenth-century old boathouse

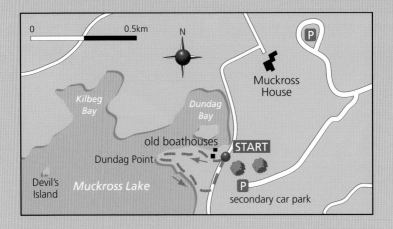

0   0.5km   N

Kilbeg
Bay

Dundag
Bay

Muckross
House

old boathouses

Dundag Point

START

Devil's
Island

Muckross Lake

secondary car park

P

The Old Boathouse Nature Trail

For those with precious little time and/or energy but who wish to experience the woodlands and lakeshore of Killarney this short walk packs in a lot. The trail is marked with limestone markers, and our notes follow them.

Start

We have the option of starting from Muckross House or driving to a car park that is close to the walk. From Muckross House car park we walk in front of the house and down towards the lake, following the signs for the Old Boathouse Nature Trail. If this walk is all that we intend to engage in then we can drive to an alternative car park: coming in the avenue from the main road we turn off the road to Muckross House, taking the first road on the left. At the end of this road there is a gravelled car park. From the car park we follow the signs for 'Boat Trips'.

Outward Journey

1. A spectacular Monterey cypress marks the start of our walk. This multi-stemmed giant with its sweeping trunks is from Monterey in California. Its delicate rounded cones can be found on the ground underneath it.
2. To our right there are two buildings in a little harbour off the lake. The one on the right is the old boathouse, for which the walk is named, and the building beside it is the new boathouse. In the old building, which dates to the nineteenth century, boats were accommodated in the water, so that they could be floated out, whereas in the new structure the boats are stored in the dry and have to be lifted and launched.
3. Here we look at the way the limestone is formed and how yew trees have colonised the area. This is Carboniferous Limestone, 300 million years old,

Monterey cypress

quite unlike the rock across the lake, which is sandstone and older by another 100 million years. The bedding planes of the limestone here are near vertical. Because limestone is soluble, over geological time, the mildly acidic waters of the lake have eroded it along its bedding planes. Thus these crevices, known as 'grykes', have been formed in which the roots of the yews find a foundation.

4. This marker is on our right. The main emphasis here is on the big yellow flowers (only in August/September) of the Rose of Sharon (*Hypericum calycinium*), a native of Greece and the Mediterranean. The pause affords us the opportunity to look at the lichen growing on the bark of the trees. There are quite a number of different lichens on view here, all of them indicators that we are in an area free of pollution. On the yew tree above the marker, the lungwort lichen proliferates.

5. This is a railed viewing point where we can see back to Muckross House. The dense woodland hides the remains of an ancient settlement. Evidence of a promontory fort and a souterrain were discovered. Piled high on the side of the trail here we notice the decaying remains of rhododendrons that have been cut. At the turn of the twenty-first century, this entire wood was being strangled by rhododendrons.

6. Dundag Point is halfway on our walk. We must walk off the trail for a few metres to reach its railed viewing point. From the Irish *dún an daig*, 'the

Lungwort lichen

Arbutus bark

wooden fort', this promontory has a fine view out into Muckross Lake. The little island we see is Devil's Island. To the right of it is Purple Mountain. Turning around to the left we see the imposing mass of Torc Mountain.

Return

7. This is the area of the arbutus trees. These wonderful trees, with their distinctive barks and red strawberry-like fruit, are not native to any other place except Mediterranean countries.

8. We have to negotiate a flight of limestone steps down to this marker. Here we make our way out to the lakeshore. Looking to our right we can see how the limestone is being eroded by the acidic waters of the lake. Back on the trail the path is through birch trees, but we notice on our left the enormous Monterey pine with its multi-stemmed base.

9. We divert off the path, following the arrow down to the Goleen shore of the lake, and walk along the shore before returning back to the path where we find the next arrow. The Killarney lakes have many species of fish, including trout and salmon, but also some rare species, such as char and shad. At the shore we can see many young Scots pines. Although these trees were once native to Ireland, they died out several millennia ago. These are from relatively recent plantations. Those near the shore are probably from cones that floated here from across the lake.

10. Meeting the main path we have reached the end of our walk and we return to Muckross, going to the left. Before doing so, however, if we walk 25 metres along the main path to the right we will see a very tall oak tree on our right. This is the evergreen oak, *Quercus ilex*, also known as the holm oak or the holly oak.

The Origin of Devil's Island

One day the chieftain O'Donoghue was up on Mangerton drinking punch with the devil out of the Devil's Punch Bowl. The two fell into an argument and O'Donoghue hit the devil a mighty blow that knocked him unconscious. Off he ran, down below Torc Waterfall to row his boat back over Muckross Lake. When the devil recovered he gave chase, but couldn't catch him. In his rage he grabbed a huge piece of the base of Torc Mountain and threw it after the chieftain. It missed and landed in the lake and it now forms Devil's Island.

Devil's Island

MUCKROSS ABBEY CIRCUIT

LENGTH:	1.5 km.
DURATION:	1½ hours.
DIFFICULTY:	Short, easy walk along a paved path. One short set of steps to descend.
INTEREST:	Walk varies from lakeshore to dense woodland. Interesting and important monastic ruin.
START/FINISH:	Car park on Muckross Road.
OPTIONS:	The steps down can be avoided by going a slightly different route. The walk can be extended into Muckross gardens. Walks 8 and 9 are very close.

Muckross Abbey

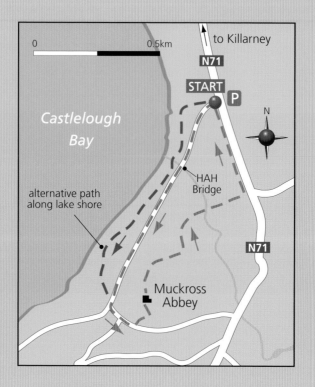

0   0.5km
to Killarney

N71

START   P

N

Castlelough
Bay

HAH
Bridge

alternative path
along lake shore

N71

Muckross
Abbey

Muckross Abbey

This walk opens with a fine stroll alongside Lough Leane. We then wander around the ruins of a monastery steeped in history, and we finish with a walk along a narrow path through dense woodland. A torch would be useful to examine the ceilings in the abbey.

Start

Leaving Killarney on the N71 towards Kenmare we cross the bridge over the Flesk River and pass hotels on either side. Two kilometres from the bridge we stop at the first public car park on our left. We cross the N71 immediately opposite the car park and proceed through the gates.

The Monastic Settlements of Killarney

Nowhere is the notion of Ireland as 'an island of saints and scholars' more poignant than here in Killarney. There were three renowned places of religious study and worship within a few miles of each other – Innisfallen, Aghadoe and Muckross. As far back as AD 600 monks came to live on the island of Innisfallen. The first church at Aghadoe dates to AD 939. Innisfallen and Aghadoe were in their final phase of religious activity when, in 1230, the Franciscan monks came to Muckross. There was a church on the site that dated to 1192 that was known as *Irrelagh* ('on the east of the lake'). Under the patronage of McCarthy Mór the Franciscans built the current church, some of it as old as 1340, but most dating to 1445. The friars were driven out several times, returning when the threats had gone, but they finally departed after Cromwellian soldiers burnt the monastery in 1652. It is said that they lived in hiding in makeshift shacks under Mangerton Mountain (known as Friar's Glen) for many years.

Outward Journey

The paved path takes us from the gates down to the shores of the lake. Below us is a narrow path that is closer to the lake and is part of the Kerry Way. We may cross over to this to get a better view. The island that we can see is Cow Island. Directly behind it, and not to be mistaken as part of it, is Rough Island. These two islands are in the part of Lough Leane known as Castlelough Bay. In order to assist with the establishment of white-tailed sea eagles an occasional culled-deer carcass is left on Rough Island for the eagles to feed on.

In the background the mountains we can see are the group that includes Shehy, Tomies and Purple. On our route we pass over a bridge that has the letters HAH carved in stone on it balustrade. This is not a laugh, but the initials of Henry Arthur Herbert, who had the bridge constructed in 1878. We have not travelled far when we notice the imposing tower of Muckross Abbey through the trees on our left.

As we round the railed corner there are some young beech trees on our left and we notice the branches heavily laden with lichens. That reinforces our perception of being out in clean air. The path comes into a copse of limes and chestnuts where we meet the avenue that takes us into the abbey.

Exploring The Abbey

Many people come to Muckross Abbey and miss its most important features. Our approach to the building is around the transept and into the nave. The nave is orientated roughly east–west, and we can follow through from it into the choir. The nave would have accommodated the lay worshippers whilst the choir would have been the reserve of the friars. The south transept was also known as Lady's Chapel.

35

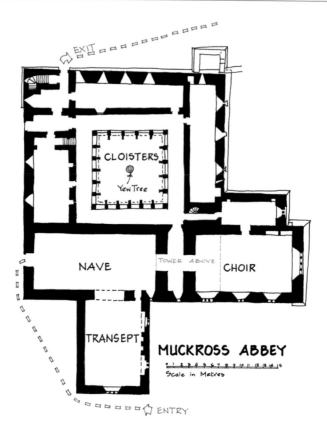

North of these places of prayer are rooms for the domestic use of the friars, including their sleeping quarters. In some of these dark rooms, if we examine the vaulted ceilings, we can understand how they were built. A curved layer of wattle and mud was used as formwork for the construction of the vaulted floor. We can see marks of the wattles in the cement matrix. Focal to the domestic friar area is the cloister court, which has an enormous yew tree in its centre. It is worth climbing the steps to the first floor where there is a small sundial and a fine limestone fireplace. We notice the diversity of construction, with Gothic and Romanesque arches and the mixture of both cut and rough limestone blocks.

Many graves are scattered around the abbey, some of which are relatively new. If we take the time we can pick out some very old graves, particularly those inside. Here are the remains of McCarthy Mór, O'Donoghue and O'Sullivan Mór as well as the graves of O'Rahilly and other Kerry poets.

Yew in the cloister court of Muckross Abbey   Exit from Muckross Abbey enclosure

Return

Outside the northeast corner of the abbey, diagonally opposite the way we came in, there is a stone opening in the boundary wall with steps externally. This opening is our return route. (The alternative way back is to return to the path we came in and follow it out to the main road, turning left to walk back to the car park).

Our path is narrow and meanders into the wood, where rhododendron is engulfing the deciduous trees. There is a stream and open parkland on our left and swampy forest on our right. Eventually we cross a very pleasant stone bridge that leads us out to the main road. We can return along the left side of the road – a short walk – to the car park.

WALK 8
THE BLUE POOL NATURE TRAIL

LENGTH:	1.5 km (circuit).
DURATION:	1 hour.
DIFFICULTY:	The path is narrow in places and is undulating, with a few steep rises and descents. There are some narrow bridges over streams and over low land.
INTEREST:	Peaceful walk through dark woodland in a swampy area rich in ferns, wild flowers and other interesting plants.
START/FINISH:	From a car park off the Mangerton Road.
OPTIONS:	The walk can be combined with the Cloghereen Nature Trail.

First narrow bridge on Blue Pool Nature Trail

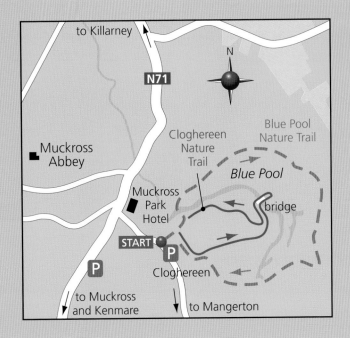

to Killarney

N71

N

Muckross
Abbey

Cloghereen
Nature
Trail

Blue Pool
Nature Trail

Blue Pool

Muckross
Park
Hotel

bridge

START

P

Cloghereen

P

to Muckross
and Kenmare

to Mangerton

The Blue Pool Nature Trail

Start

The Blue Pool and Cloghereen Nature Trails begin at the same point. Just beyond the Muckross Park Hotel and Molly Darcy's restaurant we turn left in the direction of Mangerton. Very shortly on our left we arrive at a wide gravel entrance across from a widening in the road where we can park. There is a scarcity of parking and we may have to retreat to find a space. The Blue Pool Nature Trail is a clockwise outer walk over a number of narrow bridges and it has some steep climbs and descents. The Cloghereen circuit, by contrast, is anticlockwise, shorter and flat and does not cross any of these bridges.

Hard fern   *Polypody on an oak branch*

Outward Journey

We walk in from the road and arrive at a junction in the paths. Directly ahead is the exit for both this walk and the Cloghereen Nature Trail. The path to the right, signposted as a walk for the visually impaired, is the Cloghereen Nature Trail. The path to the left that descends and crosses a narrow bridge is the Blue Pool Nature Trail.

At a bend in the trail, low on our left, we see the first of the limestone markers. We will follow these markers and pause at each.

1. If we are fortunate enough to be here in early summer the floor of the wood is covered in bluebells and dog violet flowers. The little yellow flowers are yellow pimpernel. On the branches of the oak tree above us the fern polypody has gained a foothold in the moss.

2. This marker is on the left before we reach a planked section of the walk. If we look beyond the marker we see that mighty oaks line the boundary between the forest and the field. In front of them on the left young beeches have become established. Around us the tall, slender evergreens are Sitka spruce.

    Continuing we negotiate our way over the tree roots. Perhaps we will notice the slender beech that shared the same foundation as an oak, both fighting for the same space. The oak has engulfed the beech and is now supporting its dead carcass. On the side of our walk we notice many different species of fern. The one that is most particular is the hard fern, with leaves that look like the backbone of a fish. The woodland changes to densely spaced spruce. We notice that rhododendron has a strong foothold here and we surmise that cutting it out will be necessary in the near future.

3. This marker is 20 metres short of a bridge on our left. We have entered woodland of beech, ash and alder. Along the path beyond the marker and at the foot of the hill is a giant multi-stemmed oak. As we ascend we note that

the wall is built of rounded stones. These stones are here because they were carried, rounded and eventually dropped by a glacier during the ice age. The land over which we are walking is covered in what geologists refer to as glacial till, also often referred to as boulder clay.

4. The path becomes ill defined and the marker is difficult to see. There are lots of fallen trees, these being an important ingredient in the nourishment of the ecosystem.

5. There is a steep rise followed by a steep descent and the path goes through part of the old wall. The marker is on our right. Near it is a small gravel pit in the glacial till from which stones have been taken to construct the wall. Proceeding we meet a junction in the path. If we go right we curtail the walk, so we will turn to the left.

6. Marker 6 is low on our right, partly covered. We are in an area prolific with holly. Much of the holly in Kerry has distinctive small leaves. Only the female of the species produces berries. These are an important food for birds, particularly the thrush. The rhododendrons bloom in May with flowers of a rich purple colour.

We are now halfway on our walk.

The Blue Pool, which gets its colour from minerals in the limestone

Red deer during the rutting season

Return

7. Forty metres along the track there is an arrow pointing us down to the water. Here we can see why it is called the Blue Pool Walk. The colour of the water is a light bluey-grey, due to the minerals in the limestone base. Our route now is along the bank, but we will soon be faced with a choice of direction. We may cross the little stream and follow the path beyond it, or we can decide not to cross the stream, but to turn to the left and follow a narrow, initially ill-defined track up to the main path. It is this latter route that is the designated nature trail. If our choice is to cross the stream we should read first item 10 below, which tells us about the colour of the stones in the stream.

8. This marker alerts the walker to the possibility of red deer. The deer come to the pool to drink and often their footprints or droppings can be seen.

9. We walk through a 'gate' formed by a beech and two giant Scots pines. After 30 metres we reach this marker, which is on our left. At the marker, a metre to the right, a precious oak sapling struggles to survive. The dead tree trunk that lies behind the marker has a little yew growing out of it. Twenty-five metres beyond marker 9 is a wide-canopied yew. Yew trees are either male or female, the female alone has red berries, but be careful: the berries are poisonous.

10. We must cross a bridge to arrive at this marker, which is on our left. In the stream the stones are red in colour. This is not because they are sandstone; the colour is due to algae called *Hildenbrandtia*.

11. This marker is in an area where a large oak tree fell in 2010. The oak has a hollow bark, so that its structure is merely in the outer part. If we count the rings we will discover its age when it died. If we look around we can see that ivy is trying to strangle the oaks. At the corner of the trail we pass an enclosure where black pigs are kept in a pen. These are a reminder of the wild boars that roamed these lands centuries ago, and from which the word *Torc* comes.

12. This marker is on our right. It is above a valley in the forest, the floor of which is covered in large ferns. Immediately behind the marker, beech saplings reinforce the concern that it may be beech that dominates these forests in the future.

When we arrive at the main path we turn left (not right as the marker indicates). This will take us back to the entrance. Alternatively, we can turn right and follow the Cloghereen Nature Trail. The first marker we will come to on that trail is number 4, the badger's sett.

WALK 9
THE CLOGHEREEN
NATURE TRAIL

LENGTH:	I km (circuit).
DURATION:	Less than one hour.
DIFFICULTY:	Short, easy and flat. There is a roped rail that is suitable for the visually impaired.
INTEREST:	Through woodland of oak, beech and exotic conifers, peaceful place to sit. Passing a badger's sett.
START/FINISH:	From a car park on the road to Mangerton.
OPTIONS:	For the more energetic this walk may be combined with the Blue Pool Nature Trail, which starts and finishes at the same point.

Cloghereen Pool

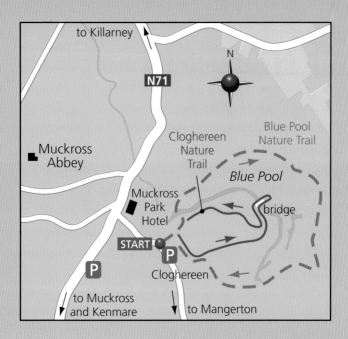

Start

The Blue Pool and Cloghereen Nature Trails begin at the same point. Just beyond the Muckross Park Hotel and Molly Darcy's restaurant we turn to the left in the direction of Mangerton. Very shortly on our left we arrive at a wide gravelled entrance across from a widening in the road where we can park. The Blue Pool Nature Trail is a clockwise outer walk over a number of narrow bridges and it has some steep climbs and descents. The Cloghereen circuit, by contrast, is anticlockwise, shorter and flatter, and does not cross any of these bridges. It is specifically set out for the visually impaired, but has many aspects of interest to all.

Walking up from the main road we arrive at a junction in the trails. Our route is to the right, and the Cloghereen Trail is confirmed by a plaque in both English and Braille. The markers here are timber posts on the roped handrail. However, many are decayed or missing.

Outward Journey

1. After just 25 metres there is a large oak to the right of the marker and a young beech on the left. Whilst the oak bark is covered in moss the smooth bark of the beech is not, because it is difficult for mosses to become established on it. Behind us, on the opposite side of the trail, there are yews surrounded by hollies.

2. At this marker we are in an area of holly. We can see that the lower leaves are much pricklier than those higher up. This deters animals from eating them.

Sitka spruce   *Western red cedar*

3. This is an area where the oak wood has been replaced with conifers. Young hollies are sprouting up, colonising the area. From here to the next marker we notice that the dreaded rhododendron is gaining a foothold.

4. We walk along, passing a steel barrier (from which the Blue Pool Nature Trail exits). Where the path bends around to the left, if we look to the right over a low bank of stones, we can see that the ground has a lack of vegetation and is disturbed. This is an area where there are badger setts. The animals come out only at night. To the left of the trail we may notice young oak saplings. While beech can grow under the tree canopy, oaks prefer open spaces. Deer rarely venture into the centre of Cloghereen and consequently oaks have the chance to regenerate.

5. A barrier crosses our path. To the left of it there is a yew tree with its branches emerging in front of Scots pines.

6. Sitka spruce trees, with their distinctive barks, are on our left, and beech trees on our right. The bark of the spruce reminds us of flaking, sunburnt skin.

7. There is a seat here in an area of spongy ground. This waterlogged area has mosses growing, the possible beginnings of a bog.

8. This is a directional marker where there is a steel barrier across the path. We are going right on a short spur down to the pond, but we will return to this junction in a few moments.

9. Before the bridge there is a picnic table, and after the bridge there is a seat on the left overlooking the Cloghereen Pool. We can hear the trickle of water long before we reach the bridge – it flows rapidly under it and there is a weir downstream of the pool. Hazel has managed to penetrate this woodland and we can see an example of it on our left as we cross the bridge.

10. The Cloghereen Pool is a peaceful place. The long branches of oaks drooping lazily into the water lend a sense of quiet repose to the spot. The pool is man-made, created as a fish hatchery and as a millpond. It attracts water birds such as ducks and moorhens.

Return

We retrace our steps back over the bridge passing the directional marker at 8.

11. At a bend in the path, on the left, close to the rope handrail, we can see that the path has been cut into the bank. The exposed soil is made up of round stones and pebbles. This is glacial till, material deposited during the ice age. Often referred to as boulder clay it is a mixture of fine silt, sand, pebbles and stones, all of them rounded as they were dragged by the ice.

12. In front of the marker is a Western hemlock. Its shape and structure is very like the Western red cedar which is more plentiful in this area. The bark of the cedar is smoother than the rough texture of the hemlock. Standing on the path we can contrast the exotic ground cover of ferns and the like in the clear, swampy ground on our right with the rather barren land under the evergreens on our left.

We now make our way out to the start of the trail.

WALK 10
CIRCUIT OF MUCKROSS LAKE

LENGTH:	10 km.
DURATION:	3 to 4 hours.
DIFFICULTY:	Easy, flat, on paved paths. During the winter and after heavy rains the path beyond Dinish Island can be flooded.
INTEREST:	This is a long walk through varied woodland. Peace and tranquillity. Geology of the Lakes of Killarney.
START/FINISH:	Muckross House.
OPTIONS:	There is a good restaurant at Muckross House and there is a cafe roughly halfway around. The Arthur Young Nature Walk covers part of this route. It is shorter.

Brickeen Bridge

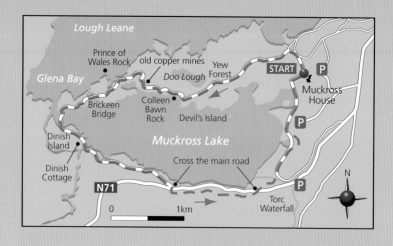

Our walk will take us initially over the blade of land that separates Lough Leane from Muckross Lake. We will cross a bridge into Dinish Island and return under Torc Mountain. We will traverse over the boundary of limestone into the older sandstone bedrock. Nowhere is erosion of the limestone more obvious than on the shores of Muckross Lake.

Start

From Muckross House we follow signs for the Colleen Bawn Rock, heading out of the clearing that is around Muckross House and into the forest.

Outward Journey

Not far along the path we are afforded the choice of going through the yew forest or taking the lake path. Our suggestion is to take a brief walk into the yew forest then return to walk along to the lakeshore. The Muckross Yew Forest is the only one of its kind in Ireland and there are only two others in Europe. The canopy provided by the yews is so complete that no vegetation except moss survives under it. It is an eerie place. There is a strange sensation of walking in the semi-darkness over a lush green carpet.

We pass stone pillars, the ruins of former buildings that supported a gate across the road, and we may notice stone markers on the left of the path. These refer to points on the Arthur Young Nature Trail (Walk No. 5). The Colleen Bawn ('white girl') Rock is an outcrop of limestone in the lake, connected to the land via a narrow causeway. We can detour down to the beach that overlooks it. A legend tells of a young girl who climbed and jumped to her death off the rock. She was broken-hearted because her lover, the son of the lord of the manor, was betrothed to another. We can see here how the limestone is being eroded by the acidic waters of the lake.

Why the Lakes of Killarney are there

The Lakes of Killarney sit between the bedrock of Devonian Old Red Sandstone and Carboniferous Limestone. The rock of the Old Red Sandstone (400 to 345 million years in age) forms the mountains of Purple and Tomies to the west. The younger limestone rock which lies to the south and east, although very hard and crystalline, is subject to solution from the mild acids that come from groundwater via the bogs and woodland that flows into the lakes. Thus, over geological time, the rock has been eroded. It is continuing to be eroded, and the lakes are gradually getting deeper.

Erosion of limestone

Yew leaves

Returning to the path our next stop is at the old gunpowder vault. This was the site of the Muckross copper mine. Across the path from it are other ruined mining buildings. Unfortunately, access to them is closed. The wood we walk through now is known as Camillan Wood. Ignoring the path to the right we proceed to Brickeen Bridge. From the bridge we can see Torc Mountain on our left and the mountains of Purple, Tomies and Shehy straight ahead. The only outlet from Muckross Lake to Lough Leane is at Brickeen Bridge. During heavy rainfall the level of water under the bridge can rise dramatically.

Our path takes us over a narrow causeway into Dinish Island. At Dinish Cottage (Dinish is pronounced locally *dynis*) we can rest and have a drink in the cafe.

Return

Dinish Island is renowned for its azaleas. In front of Dinish Cottage (down near the public toilets) we can stand at the edge of the water and look up the river that connects the Upper Lake to Muckross Lake (known as the Long Range) to see Old Weir Bridge with its distorted arches. This area is the Meeting of the Waters.

Toothache Bridge

The bridge that connects Dinish Island to the mainland is known locally as Toothache Bridge. It is a low, timber bridge, with the water flowing close to its soffit so that it is generally possible to kneel on the bridge and touch the water. If the folklore is to be believed then he who wets his teeth by dipping and rubbing his finger will never have to endure a toothache.

Boats from the Upper Lake have to negotiate the rapids under the bridge.

From Dinish Island we proceed out to the main road. During periods of heavy rain the path here can be flooded. The predominant trees in this stretch are oaks, with just the occasional yew and holly. At the main road we cross over and take the path through the wood under Torc Mountain. Here the rhododendrens have a stranglehold, threatening to engulf the few yews that remain. The undulating path rises and falls, but it provides us with fine views over Muckross Lake, with the spire of St Mary's Cathedral in the distance. When the path comes back down to the main road, opposite a car park, we cross the road again and follow the signs for Muckross House.

Old Weir Bridge

WALK 11
TORC WATERFALL CIRCUIT

In the Torc waterfall area there is a choice of three walks, all of them marked out by Killarney National Park, two of which are moderate and will take less than one hour (the blue and yellow walks). The third walk is much longer and challenging, and this is the one set out below. It is the one which Killarney National Park has marked out in red.

LENGTH: 5 km.

DURATION: 2 to 3 hours.

DIFFICULTY: This is a strenuous walk, not for the faint-hearted. There are lots of very steep steps to climb and to descend. Hiking boots, to protect our ankles, are recommended. A walking stick will be useful for our descent, which is very steep in places.

INTEREST: Torc Waterfall is a 'must see' of Killarney. Great views over Muckross Lake. Possibly encounter sika deer in the rhododendron areas.

START/FINISH: A car park beyond Torc Waterfall.

OPTIONS: The walk can be extended over to Dinish Island which would add 3 km to the distance.

Killarney National Park requires walkers to follow the red markers in an anticlockwise direction, so that on the steep climbs we do not have to meet walkers coming in the opposite direction. This means we will not come to the waterfall until towards the end of the walk. For this walk there is no cafe en route, no place to purchase water or food. However, there is a wonderful spot at the top of the walk to sit and have a picnic.

Start

Taking the N71 in the direction of Kenmare we travel 2 km beyond Muckross House and 0.5 km past Torc Waterfall. The first car park beyond Torc Waterfall is on the right-hand side of the road and we can park here under the trees.

Outward Journey

We must cross the main road onto the path on the other side and turn to the right to follow the signs for Dinis Cottage. Our path is under Torc Mountain and runs above and parallel to the road. The National Park intends to clear out all the rhododendron eventually, and they recognise that their biggest task is Torc Mountain. We can see how effective this foreign invader is in engulfing and

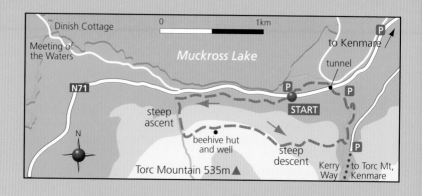

Torc Waterfall

Torc Waterfall

*Beehive hut and well at the top of the
Torc Waterfall walk*

strangling the native species. Our trail is undulating and we have fine views over the lake. After a kilometre we must be careful to find the path up to our left. It is before the main path drops to the road. Should we wish to extend the walk we can drop down to cross the road and make our way out to Dinish Island, which has a cafe that is open during the summer months.

We climb the steep purpose-made stairway, holding on to the roped handrail. It is here that we see the wisdom of making the walk a one-way circuit. We are climbing up a geological fault. Torc Mountain sits on 400-million-year-old Devonian Sandstone. Around Muckross Lake below us the base rock is Carboniferous Limestone, some of it 100 million years younger. When both strata were deposited the younger rock obviously sat on top of the older rock. Soon after the limestone was deposited, a period of tectonic-plate collision occurred when the land under Torc was lifted up 3,000 metres. We are climbing the fault line of that upheaval, known as the Muckross to Millstreet Fault Line. Further along the walk we will pass areas where we can see that the bedding planes of the rock are horizontal, confirming that the land was lifted, rather than being burst and turned.

At the top of the steps the path winds around to the left and east, and our views down to Muckross Lake are finer. After we go over the highest point and begin to descend we come across a stone well in the middle of our route. There is a chain with a cup attached for those who are brave enough to drink. Immediately beside the well is a stone beehive shelter with stone seats. This, or one of the spurs off the path further on, makes a fine area to rest and picnic.

Return

Although we have the luxury of going downhill all the way to the finish we must be careful on the steep descents. Our stone path was constructed in 2010/2011 and follows the route of an old path that was muddy and slippery. The trail eventually emerges to cross via a bridge over the river that feeds the waterfall. This is the Owengarriff River whose source is the Devil's Punch Bowl up on Mangerton Mountain.

Our descent follows the plunging river until we meet another stone stairway. At its base we have the full vista of Torc Waterfall. Its water sprays over enormous rounded boulders in the river. If we are fortunate to have come after a period of wet weather the falls are at their most spectacular.

We continue to descend, passing Scots pines shrouded in a blanket of rich, green moss. When we arrive at the building that houses public toilets we pass close by it and our route is through the tunnel under the main road. Emerging from the tunnel we follow the path that circles around to the left. This will take us through a gate when we will be looking over pastureland towards Muckross Lake. Our route is to the left, crossing an old stone bridge and following the path back to the car park.

WALK 12
TORC MOUNTAIN

LENGTH:	9 km.
DURATION:	3 to 4 hours.
DIFFICULTY:	Very gradual mountain climb. The path is either stony or is over timber planks. Boots are desirable though the majority climb in simple runners.
INTEREST:	The walk is initially through a dense forest then out over mountain moorland. Wonderful views over the lakes. Possibility of seeing deer.
START/FINISH:	A car park on the road to Kenmare.
OPTIONS:	The walk may be commenced at a higher car park which reduces the length by 3km and the time by up to an hour. The walk may be combined with the Torc Waterfall Walk.

The climb of Torc Mountain is a most suitable introduction to hillwalking

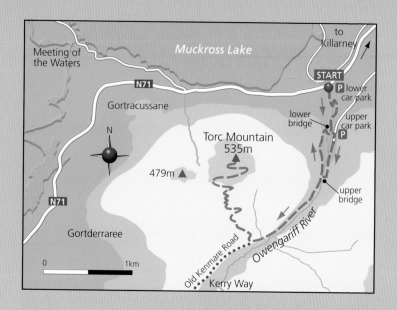

If there was ever an ideal mountain to introduce children to hillwalking then Torc Mountain would have to be top of the list. The path is relatively free of mud, being either stony, paved with boulders or over wooden planks wrapped in chicken wire. The gradient is low and there are few dangers on the route.

Start

We will start our walk at the car park for Torc Waterfall, and we will pass the waterfall en route to the summit. However, we have the option of avoiding the lower part of the walk and driving up to a higher car park that will shorten our journey. For the shorter option we take the first road to the left beyond the main gate to Muckross House and Gardens. For the longer option we park at the Torc Waterfall car park and walk up to the waterfall. Our path is the stepped stone stairway that continues after the waterfall. We will arrive at a junction in the path where we can see below us a bridge (the Lower Bridge on our map) over the river that feeds the waterfall, and note that our return route will be over that bridge. Ignoring the path to the bridge we rise to meet the old Killarney to Kenmare Road that is part of the Kerry Way. Had we taken the shorter option we would park at this point.

On the path we will have passed areas where the dreaded rhododendron is being cleared. We see how it engulfs the forest, with only tall pines able to shoot up through them.

View from the summit of Torc Mountain

Torc

The word Torc comes from the Gaelic for 'wild boar'. This is suggestive of its hunting traditions. The summit has an altitude of 535 metres. The altitude of the car park on the main road is a mere 55 metres, so that the total climb is 480 metres. The land on which the mountain is today was raised in an enormous earthquake 290 million years ago. The fault that occurred then lifted the land up 3,000 metres. The side of the mountain that faces Muckross Lake was once a sheer vertical face. Over geological time it has been eroded to the steep incline that it shows today.

Outward Journey

We follow signs for the Kerry Way to the Black Valley, crossing a bridge with wooden rails (the Upper Bridge on our map) and turning to our left. The path takes us up through a forest of pines and oaks to emerge eventually onto open moorland. This initial part of the walk is the steepest section, and once we have completed it the gradient becomes gentler. We reflect that this was once the main road from Killarney to Kenmare when donkeys and carts would ply up and down this hill.

Where the path flattens out we see the blue sign on our right that indicates the path up Torc Mountain. The path zigs and zags on a gentle gradient, over stone and timber planks, and there are many false summits before we finally reach the exposed rocky top. Below us, on a clear day, is the expanse of the Killarney lakes, with the town off to our right. If we look around to our left, passing the mountains of Purples and Tomies, we can see down through the Black Valley. Above and slightly to the right of the Black Valley lake is Carrauntoohil, the highest peak in Ireland. It appears to stand out on its own. To the left of it we see the hump of Caher, the third highest mountain in Ireland. Behind us is Mangerton Mountain, which is all of 300 metres higher than Torc.

Return

We return down the mountain by the route we came up, and we are tempted by the many shortcuts we now notice. Our hosts, the Killarney National Park, would prefer us to stay on the designated path. This is to contain the erosion caused by walkers. As we descend we can see, across the valley, stones from ruined structures. This is Core's Hill, where farm buildings existed during the period of the old Kenmare to Killarney Road. When the new road was constructed, many homesteads were removed to make way for lucrative hunting. Those times are known as 'the Clearances'.

When we arrive at the bridge with the wooden handrail we take the left-hand path to return to the waterfall via a different route. At the next path junction we go right, and at the next junction we also go right to cross the bridge over the river that feeds the falls. This is the Owengarriff River. Its source is Mangerton, where one of its tributaries comes out of the lake of the Devil's Punch Bowl.

Planked section of the Torc Mountain walk

WALK 13
LORD BRANDON'S COTTAGE AND RETURN BY BOAT

LENGTH:	Taxi to car park above Torc Waterfall, 14 km walk to Lord Brandon's cottage, returning from there by boat to Killarney.
DURATION:	Day trip. 4-hour walk. 1½-hour boat trip.
DIFFICULTY:	Partly over a rough path, stepping from stone to stone, some relatively hard inclines. Hiking boots recommended. Relaxing ride home. Binoculars could be useful for sightings of eagles.
INTEREST:	Long walk in varied countryside, back into history, passing giant oaks, cascades, finishing with a wonderful boat ride, as enjoyed by Queen Victoria in 1861.
START/FINISH:	Killarney Town.
OPTIONS:	Curtail the walk by starting at Derrycunnihy Church, reducing the walk distance to 4 km. By starting at Torc Waterfall and climbing up to the higher car park we can extend the walk by an hour. Nice restaurant at Lord Brandon's Cottage. Take the Gap of Dunloe walk ending at Lord Brandon's Cottage and take the boat trip home.

This walk follows the old Kenmare Road, then branches off to descend to the Upper Lake. Seeing the essential sights of Killarney should include a boat trip. By far the best trip by boat is from Lord Brandon's Cottage, which takes passengers through the Upper Lake, along the river channel known as the Long Range, through Muckross Lake and into Lough Leane. Because this boat trip is a scheduled one it is relatively inexpensive.

Start
Our start must be timed so that we meet the boat that departs from Lord Brandon's Cottage every day at 2.15 p.m. (we must check that the timetable has not been changed. Out of season we must check if the boat trip is possible). A taxi from town to the upper car park at Torc will take half an hour. The walk from there to Lord Brandon's Cottage will take 4 hours, so that, to ensure we have time for lunch, we must depart Killarney at 9.00 a.m. For those of us on a slower pace this time may need to be earlier.

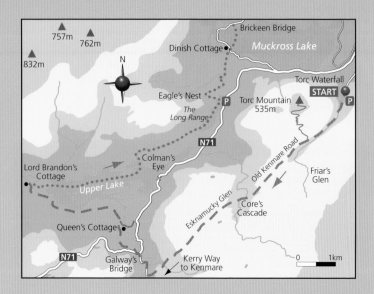

Outward Journey

From the car park above Torc Waterfall we take the Kerry Way in the direction of Kenmare. This is the Old Kenmare Road. Until the early part of the eighteenth century the only connection between Killarney and Kenmare was a track over the mountainous terrain. The track was developed into a more passable road in the mid-1750s when ore from Muckross was taken to Kenmare for export. As we walk we will see evidence of old homesteads on either side.

Our walk begins in varied woodland and we marvel at the depth of moss that clothes every tree bark. When we have climbed out of the woodland and gained the open moorland we must watch out for deer. Just beyond where there is a path up to Torc Mountain, we notice, on our left, the ruins of a homestead and old field boundaries. The people living here were relocated to make way for hunting during the era of 'the Clearances'. The river we have been walking alongside, the Owengarriff, now turns up towards Mangerton into an area known as Friar's Glen. During and after the Cromwell era, the friars, forced to flee Muckross Abbey, were known to have had a hideout here.

Thankfully, the dreaded rhododendron is absent from this area of Killarney. We will only meet it as we approach Galway's River further on. As we descend the slope before Core's Cascade we notice the fields on either side have been stripped of boulders to allow cultivation. The presence of these rounded boulders, of which we will see more on our right further on, tells us that they are

Boarding at Lord Brandon's Cottage

glacial deposits. During an ice age a glacier pushed through the valley of Upper Lake and the Long Range, depositing this glacial moraine on its flank. The road narrows to a track as we walk through Esknamucky Glen. As we rise out of the glen we reflect on the hardship of those using the road trying to get horses and donkeys to negotiate these steep rocks. The path out of the glen is planked where the ground is boggy.

When we reach a paved path we leave the Kenmare Road to turn right in the direction of the Black Valley. This path takes us up to the N71 at Galway's Bridge. Here the Galway River flows through the Derrycunnihy Cascade down into Upper Lake. We cross the road and follow the sign for the Black Valley, descending through a woodland of giant oaks. On the right of the path there is one tree with a double trunk, perched atop an enormous boulder. At the base of the wood we reach a path coming from our right. This was a carriageway built by the Herberts for Queen Victoria's visit. It afforded the royal party a relatively flat drive from Lord Brandon's Cottage (where they departed by boat) around the shore of the lake to view the Derrycunnihy Cascade. If we turn right on this path for a few steps we will see the ruins of an old cottage. Known as 'Queen's Cottage' this was specifically built so that the royal party could have refreshments.

Continuing our journey we walk along the lakeshore to Lord Brandon's Cottage. William Crosbie, Lord Brandon (1771–1832), built a hunting lodge here. It is now in ruins and has a rather modern round tower on the site. There is a restaurant nearby where we can purchase our ticket for the boat.

Oak wood approaching Galway's Bridge   *Bridge in Esknamucky*

Return

In 2011 the scheduled departure time every day from May to September was 2.15 p.m. There are no boats after this time, and hiring a taxi will be rather expensive, so we must be attentive to the time.

The boat travels down the narrow river and emerges into Upper Lake. We notice that every one of the small islands in the Lakes of Killarney has a name, and many have a story behind the name. Ronayne's Island is called after a recluse who, in the early nineteenth century, made a permanent camp there, cutting himself off from the rest of the world. However, he became a tourist attraction, and boats would circle the island to catch a view of the unfortunate fellow. And so, fed up with being spied upon, one day he vanished, probably to find a more secluded place elsewhere. Arbutus Island has indeed many fine arbutus trees growing on it, though no junipers can be spotted on Juniper Island.

The only exit out of Upper Lake is via Colman's Eye, a narrow passage between the rocks through which the boat barely passes. As we move along

In Royal Footsteps

The British Royal family's enchantment with Killarney begins in 1858, when the seventeen-year-old Prince of Wales, later to become King Edward VII, visited. He spent some time here and amongst his exploits he climbed Carrauntoohil. The guidebooks that became so popular after his visit tell us that he placed a stone on the summit cairn, and suggested that other climbers do likewise. Queen Victoria came in 1861 and stayed at Muckross House. In 1897 the Prince of Wales returned. Following his second visit negotiations began for the purchase of Muckross House as a royal residence. There are many place names that refer to these visits – Queen's Drive, Ladies View, Queen's Cottage, Prince of Wales Drive.

the Long Range we notice the smoothness of the rocks, formed by the ice-age glacier grinding its way through. In the early twentieth century there were eagles on Eagles Nest. The boatman would stop the boat and discharge a shotgun to disturb the birds for the benefit of the tourists (how environmentally unfriendly we were in those days!).

We will all have to disembark approaching Old Weir Bridge and walk down past the bridge to re-embark. This is because the water is shallow and there are rapids at the bridge. Below the bridge we are in The Meeting of the Waters where the waters from the Upper Lake meet those of Muckross Lake. On our left we see a house. This is Dinish Cottage, now a cafe, formerly a hunting lodge. We pass under a wooden bridge that separates Dinish Island (pronounced *dynis*) from the mainland. Under this, Toothache Bridge; if we dip our finger in the water and rub it over our teeth it is said that we will never again suffer a toothache.

The boat inches under the very ancient Brickeen Bridge and out into Lough Leane. The water can be rough here, so that seats near the rear of the boat will be drier. The long island on our right is Rough Island where eagles are often sighted. We must round Ross Island to gain the protection of Innisfallen Island when the water will be calmer again. After seventy-five minutes on the boat our journey's end is Ross Castle.

Return of the Eagles

The Killarney area had a population of eagles until they died out at the beginning of the twentieth century. There are two 'Eagles' Nest' place names – one above the Long Range and the other on the side of Carrauntoohil. In 2007 a project was set up to reintroduce the eagles from Scotland. The first white-tailed sea eagles were released over Lough Leane in 2007 and more birds have been released since then. The birds have been sighted as far north as Galway. Around Lough Leane and up over the mountains are the best potential sites to see them. There is a website that provides information and where sightings are recorded: www. goldeneagle.ie

WALK 14
THE BLACK VALLEY CIRCUIT

LENGTH:	13 km.
DURATION:	3½ hours.
DIFFICULTY:	Undulating. A short part of the walk is over a rough path that can be wet; the remainder is on a paved road.
INTEREST:	Wild, secluded country walk through a valley, passing lakes and with high mountains on either side.
START/FINISH:	Black Valley Church.
OPTIONS:	The walk may be combined with all or part of the walk through the Gap of Dunloe. Lord Brandon's Cottage, which has a restaurant, is on the route in to the Black Valley.

Jarvey in the Black Valley

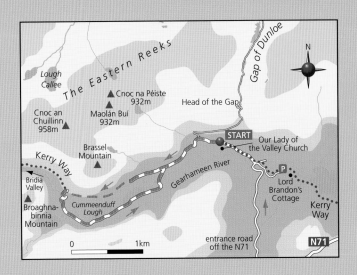

During the summer jarveys take their jaunting cars through the Gap of Dunloe and cars are distinctly frowned upon. Accessing this walk therefore, from April to October, should always be from the N71 and Moll's Gap. The drive from Moll's Gap itself is an adventure into wild countryside. It is highly likely that the traveller will not meet a soul on the drive or on the walk through the Black Valley.

Start

We drive out the N71 Muckross Road towards Kenmare, under the tunnel, passing Galway's Bridge and Ladies View, up to the road junction of Moll's Gap. Turning right towards Sneem we will not go far until we take the first road on our right. On this narrow, winding road we must go right at the first junction and left at the second, taking us past Lord Brandon's Cottage, then past a hostel to the Black Valley Church. We can park at the church.

Outward journey

Passing the Black Valley Church we come to a Y-junction and follow the cul-de-sac sign and the Kerry Way. For half of our walk we will travel the Kerry Way, following marker posts. At this Y-junction we have the option of making a detour by turning right and climbing up the road to the Head of the Gap where we can look down into the Gap of Dunloe.

The Black Valley is sheep-grazing country. If we have come in April it is lambing season when the ewes are brought in from the mountains to give birth. Very old hawthorns, birches and hollies eventually give way to the dreaded rhododendron, which has a firm foothold in this part of the Black Valley.

Father Sears and the men of the Black Valley head off for a day on the construction of the new church in 1955

Our Lady of the Valley Church

A Church Physically Built by the People

The Church of our Lady of the Valley was built in the 1950s by the people of the Black Valley. Motivated by their priest, Father Sears, the men would regularly be collected in a tractor to build the structure. This fine church is a monument to the dedication of these people and to their sense of place.

As we walk deeper into the valley we notice the mountain on our right. This is Brassel Mountain. It is smooth and rounded on the left and serrated on the right. This is an example of a *roche moutonnée*. During the ice age an enormous glacier moved up through the Black Valley, smoothing the mountains in its path. The serrated side of Brassel faced away from the direction of the glacier. As the ice passed it tore rocks off the back of the mountain. If we look beyond Brassel there is a mountain with a distinctive geological fault line in it. This is Cnoc an Chuillinn. The land on the right has dropped with respect to that on the left of the fault. Cnoc an Chuillinn hides Ireland's highest mountain, Carrauntoohil, from our view.

At the end of the paved road we follow the signs through the gate. On this part of the walk we will have to climb over two ladder stiles in order to pass over fences. It is safer to climb up to the platform and then to turn and step down backwards.

Passing through a tree plantation of spruce and pine we emerge to a vista of the end of the valley. The mountain that appears to block the Black Valley is Broaghnabinnia. The Kerry Way, from which we will shortly deviate, continues around Broaghnabinnia into the Bridia Valley beyond our view. After we pass a house and begin to descend we come to a paved road and we turn left. This paved road will take us back to the church.

Return

The road drops down to the floor of the valley passing gnarled old holly trees. As we emerge near the lakeshore – Lough Cummeenduff – we stop and look up to our right. There is an enormous waterfall in the distance. The water is the Gearhameen River, which has flowed out of a corrie lake (Lough Reagh). It is joined by the Cummeenduff River flowing around Broaghnabinnia, and the combined river fills the lakes of the Black Valley. If we look now into the valley around Broaghnabinnia we can see the Kerry Way snaking up the hillside.

Acidic run-off from the land generates algae over the rocks in the lakes to colour their surfaces black. This is where the valley gets its name. In the wet lowlands of the valleys in early summer we may spot delicate wild orchids.

Approaching the second lake we can see ahead of us the impressive mass of Purple Mountain. Rejoining the road when we originally entered the valley we turn right to go back to the church.

Walkers in the Black Valley with Brassel Mountain to the right

View of Purple Mountain from the Black Valley

WALK 15
MANGERTON MOUNTAIN CIRCUIT

LENGTH:	10 km.
DURATION:	4 to 5 hours.
DIFFICULTY:	A relatively strenuous climb. The lower part can be wet and muddy. Waterproof boots are essential.
INTEREST:	Wonderful views. Walk through an ancient battle site. Possibility of seeing deer and eagles.
START/FINISH:	A car park off the road to Kenmare.
OPTIONS:	The walk may be curtailed at the Devil's Punch Bowl. The summit is uninteresting unless we want to bag a peak.

The Devil's Punchbowl on Mangerton Mountain

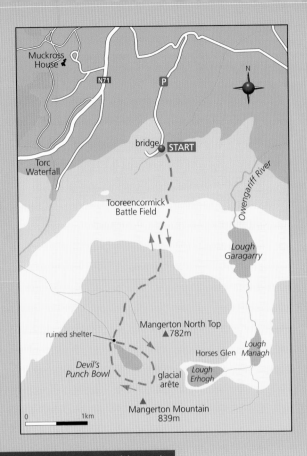

Mangerton Mountain

The place names on this walk are evocative – *The Devil's Punch Bowl, Horses Glen*, even *Mangerton* itself. And the walk does not disappoint. Mangerton Mountain is one of the most popular climbs in Ireland, because it is challenging, yet presents no great difficulty. There is no scrambling involved, no clambering over dangerous rocks. It is a steady walk all the way, and should be OK for anyone who is reasonably fit.

Start

We leave Killarney on the N71 for Kenmare. Pass the Lake Hotel, then the Muckross Lodge Hotel and Molly Darcy's where there is a road junction with a sign for Mangerton. We follow the signs to eventually come along a flat road with a pine forest on our right and open ground on our left. There is a linear, gravelled car park where we can park. The starting point for the climb is half a kilometre further along and we may drive to it to see if there is any parking available. The road is a cul-de-sac.

Fingerpost sign for Mangerton

The Battle of Tooreencormick 1262

It was the period when the Normans were trying to establish a foothold in this part of Kerry, but they were being fiercely resisted by the MacCarthys. In 1261 Fingen MacCarthy ambushed the Normans and killed their leader, John FitzThomas FitzGerald. When Fingen died, his brother Cormac continued the fight. But there was no ambush on this occasion. Cormac's army soundly defeated the Normans on this piece of boggy heath. The battles of Callan in 1261 and Tooreencormick in 1262 put an end to the Norman incursion, and a long period of peace followed. The battle site is named after Cormac.

Outward Journey

At a bend in the road there is a small bridge over a stream leading to the path that will take us up the mountain. We must negotiate through a muddy area before we start our climb, and when we are out of the mud we will pause and reflect. We are now in the middle of a former battlefield.

As we climb we should note that the mountain on our left is unfortunately not our goal. It is the northern peak of Mangerton and has an elevation of 782 metres, 63 metres short of the main summit. Where the path crosses a stream there is a branch path to our left, which we should ignore. It also rises to our destination, but the path is very boggy. As we climb we get our first glimpse of the Mangerton summit. The corrie lake we arrive at is known as the Devil's Punch Bowl. On the left of the path, immediately at the mouth of the lake, there are the remains of a ruined shelter. This was formerly a gamekeeper's hut. As we follow the path to the left to skirt the lake we come to further ruins that indicate the popularity of the place for hunting.

Return

There is a path that circles the corrie lake. We must deviate off this path if we want to get to the summit. If attaining the summit is not important to us then we should at least go to the point where we can peer over the glacial arête to gaze into Horses Glen. Below us is Lough Erhogh and beyond that Lough Managh. The mountain high above Lough Managh is Stoompa. We are looking into a period of prehistory when a volcano erupted through the surface. Four hundred million years ago the period of the Killarney Traps occurred. Pyroclastic ash covered the ground we are standing on. Beyond Lough Managh the Horses Glen follows into Lough Garagarry. Here the volcanic heat and upheaval turned layers of shale into slate, which was quarried in the last century for roofing slate.

After circling the Devil's Punch Bowl we retrace our steps back down to the starting point. Punch is a mixture of whiskey, sugar and hot water, often also spiced up with cloves. It is said that the devil sits around his punch bowl inviting walkers to sip, so we will be wary!

The delicate bog asphodel will be seen in the wet land at the foot of Mangerton. The flower, which flourishes in late summer, was also known in the old days as 'Maiden Hair' because young women collected it in order to dye their hair.

WALK 16
HAG'S GLEN CIRCUIT

LENGTH:	5 km.
DURATION:	2½ hours.
DIFFICULTY:	Some gradual inclines, but mostly flat. The route is partially over boggy ground that requires waterproof boots. This is not a suitable walk for a wet day: the mountain views would be hidden and there are many slippery rocks to cross.
INTEREST:	The glen is renowned the world over as the base for those climbing Ireland's highest peaks. On the circuit we will see interesting mountain features and many of Ireland's hidden flora and fauna.
START/FINISH:	Cronin's Yard.
OPTIONS:	There is a nice, friendly cafe in Cronin's Yard. We can avoid the climb and the boggy ground by staying at a low level on the outward journey. The walk can be extended by 7 km out to Lisleibane.

This is a walk in mountain wilderness. The route varies in elevation from 60 metres to 320 metres, but towering above it are peaks that reach over 1,000 metres. We have now left Killarney National Park and we walk over private property. The owners of the lands have always recognised the recreational importance of these mountains and we are indebted to them for their continuing permission. There are plans to lay planks over the boggy areas.

Start

Taking the N72 from Killarney towards Killorglin we pass the district of Fossa, and we take the signposted road to the left towards Glencar. Along this road we will pass a road to our left for the Gap of Dunloe. Further on we pass a road junction known as Kissane's Cross (there is a small shop there owned by the Kissanes). Immediately beyond the crossroads we take the first left, which is signposted Carrauntoohil and Cronin's Yard. We drive to the end of this road and enter the Cronin's Yard car park. Our route into Hag's Glen is signposted Carrauntoohil.

Hag's Glen

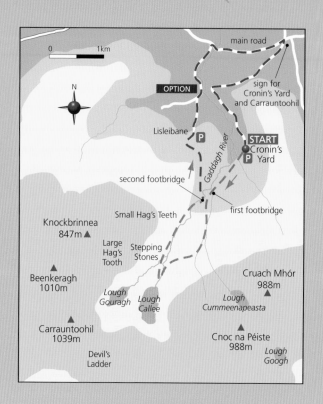

Cronin's Yard

Mountaineers the world over will be familiar with Cronin's Yard. The starting point for walking the MacGillycuddy's Reeks has been in the Cronin family for hundreds of years. In the cafe there are pictures of the generations of owners of the yard. John Cronin, the current owner, is a prominent mountaineer and a member of Kerry Mountain Rescue. The cafe not only serves great coffee but exudes a friendly atmosphere.

Mythical Placenames

The place names of the area are steeped in mythology, most particularly relating to witches, devils and serpents. The hag of the glen was an old witch who also laid claim to the lake nearest the Eastern Reeks, Lough Callee ('the hag's lake'). The most popular route up Carrauntoohil is via the Devil's Ladder. Knocknapeasta translates as the 'hill of the serpent'.

The Hag's Tooth (right) with a snow-covered Carrauntoohil beyond it

Outward Journey

We leave the yard on a winding track with fences on either side. As we enter the glen we can see the sharp outline of Carrauntoohil directly ahead. At 1,039 metres it is Ireland's highest and toughest peak. In the foreground there is an odd-shaped projection from a mountain. This is the Hag's Tooth. On our journey we cross a green pedestrian bridge and we meet the first of the signposts that will mark our route. We are following the purple track designated the Cronin's Yard Loop. We cross a fence using a 'stile', noting that we are advised to turn at the top and step down backwards. At the next signpost we are directed uphill to our left. However, for those short of the energy for a climb, there is the option of going straight, following along the bank of the river. The signposted uphill route does

Hag's Glen marker

not go very high and stops well short of the mountains we see, which are known as the Eastern Reeks. The first of these has a structure at its pinnacle. This is Cruach Mhór ('the big stack'). The structure, several metres in height, was constructed by one man over a number of years, ascending religiously to its summit day after day to build his monument of stone. The next peak after Cruach Mhór is Cnoc na Péiste, the fourth highest of the MacGillycuddy's Reeks at 988 metres. Between the peaks of Cruach Mhór and Cnoc na Péiste, and out of view, is a corrie lake. Its face appears like a dam stretching across from the two mountains with a stream trickling from it. In 1943 an American DC transport plane that had wandered off course on a stormy night crashed into Cnoc na Péiste and its broken remains were strewn over the mountain and the lake. On a clear day one of its wings can be seen at the bottom of the corrie lake.

Our route soon begins to drop back to the river, where we turn left up towards Lough Callee. Here we must carefully hop from stone to stone to cross the shallow waters that are the start of the River Gaddagh. We will rise to meet a stony path and turn right for the route back.

From Lough Callee if we look up to our left we can see into the fold in the mountains that is known as Eisc na bhFiach ('the fissure of the ravens'). From Carrauntoohil there is a narrow ridge that connects to the smooth-topped Beenkeragh ('the peak of the sheep'), Ireland's second highest mountain. Closer to us the jagged peak in the foreground is Stumpa an tSaimh (the stump of the sorrel).

Return

Our return journey is along a relatively flat stony path that follows the river. We can now see the full view of the Hag's Tooth, with the mountain of Knockbrinnea behind it.

We watch out for pieces of bog oak, stumps of old trees that were engulfed in the bog. We should also see many examples of bog cotton and we may be lucky to see bog orchids or bog asphodels. Hag's Glen is renowned for its frogs. The frogs lay their spawn in February, and by early summer the young frogs have emerged into the moorland. The most popular high-flying birds are the black ravens, though kestrels, falcons and even white-tailed sea eagles may also be seen. The meadow pipit is the most popular small bird.

On the way home we must cross the river that emerges from Lough Gouragh ('the lake of the goats'), this time stepping from stone to stone. Further along, as we begin to climb up out of the valley, we make a right turn to descend to the river and cross the second green steel bridge. We have the option of extending our walk by following the signs for Lisleibane. This will take us to a car park. We can walk from the car park out to the main road, turn right and come back into Cronin's Yard.

Stepping stones in Hag's Glen　　　　*Stumpa an tSaimh*

WALK 17
CIRCUIT OF TOMIES WOOD

LENGTH:	9.5 km.
DURATION:	3 hours.
DIFFICULTY:	Gently sloping gravel path. No requirement for special footwear. Since it is necessary to walk through a private farm dogs are not allowed on this walk.
INTEREST:	Quiet walk through mature woods. Waterfall as impressive as Torc. Good views over the lake with Killarney in the background. Sika deer. Giant oaks.
START/FINISH:	Off a secluded road in the district of Beaufort.
OPTIONS:	A shorter walk direct to the waterfall and back is 6 km. Walk extension to Benson's Point adds a further 1.5 km. Refreshments in Kate Kearney's Cottage – a public house and restaurant.

Tomies Wood is a deciduous wood at the base of Tomies Mountain. Deer (mainly sika deer) frequent the wood and the surrounding lands. Even though it has a rather long initial incline it is a popular circuit for joggers. En route we will pass a waterfall that is every bit as spectacular as Torc Waterfall.

Start

To reach the start of this walk we drive out of Killarney taking the N72 towards Killorglin. Driving through the district of Fossa we take the next road on our left signposted to Glencar (and the Gap of Dunloe). The road crosses a bridge and further on comes to a sharp right-hand bend. We take the narrow road to the left at this bend, which is signposted Lough Leane. This road is a cul-de-sac. Near its end, and just before it bends to the left over a concrete bridge, we will find a parking place. Our walk is the dirt track that continues straight alongside the river.

Outward Journey

We follow the lane through a working farm, through several pedestrian gates, opening and closing a gate behind us. This is a right of way that leads us over private land into the National Park. A wooden bridge takes us into the wood, where we come to a junction in the trail and we have the choice of going left (signposted O'Sullivan's Cascade) or right. We will take the option to go right, thus getting the climbing over with at an early stage. The gorse here is very old and reaches a great height.

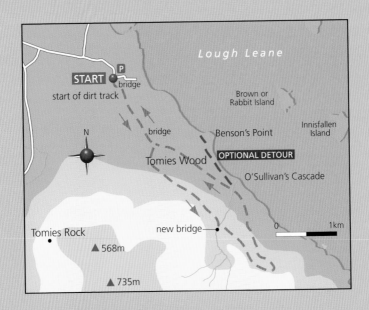

Tomies Wood

Tomies Wood

Gorse in full bloom in mid-May

Tomies view

The Legend of the Whiskey Spring

In ancient times the chieftain of the area, O'Sullivan Mhór, was hunting deer when he met the great warrior, Fionn Mac Cumhaill. An altercation between the two, who happened to be hunting the same stag, was avoided when Mac Cumhaill offered to provide the chieftain with a drink. Digging his heel into the ground Fionn caused a spring to appear out of which spurted uisce beatha, the water of life – whiskey. The spring continued to ooze whiskey until the Normans invaded Ireland when the whiskey turned to water.

As we near the first corner we notice that the larch and birch trees are dripping with lichen, which tells us we are in an area of unpolluted air. Around the corner we soon can catch glimpses of the lake with Killarney beyond it. Be patient: our view of it will be quite spectacular further on. The trees here are quite a mixture, with silver birch, holly and beech prominent, and oaks, pines and spruce sparse. On the trunks of the oaks we see that the fern polypody is growing out of the moss.

We reach a vantage point where we have a clear view over the lake below us with Ross Castle on the far side. When we reach the bridge over the river (a rather unnecessarily imposing structure in this isolated area), the path has flattened and it is downhill virtually all the way from here. At the end of the loop we notice that rhododendron has a significant foothold. Be alert in this area for sika deer. They like the shelter that the rhododendron provides.

Return

As we approach the bridge and O'Sullivan's Cascade we notice the holly trees, with their white, gnarled barks. These trees are very old and have distinctive small leaves.

The Royal Oak, said to be the largest oak in Killarney.

It is well worth the effort to follow the signs and descend the steps to O'Sullivan's Cascade. The waterfall is a fine sight. We have the option now of extending our trip by continuing down the sloping path past O'Sullivan's Cascade. It will take us to the lakeshore, between giant oaks, to Benson's Point. However, we only consider this if we want the exercise or we want a view over the lake, for the same giant oaks will also be seen on our return to the start of the walk. Benson's Point can be a good vantage point to look out for eagles over the lake. Down near the lakeshore there is a giant oak, known as the Royal Oak. It is said to be the largest oak in Killarney. Unfortunately, the rhododendrons block our path to it and it can be viewed only from a boat on the lake.

We make our way back out to complete the loop and proceed back to the public road. For lunch or refreshments we are not far from Kate Kearney's Cottage in the Gap of Dunloe.

How Old are the Oak Trees?

Most of the oak trees in this area of Killarney date from the early to the middle part of the nineteenth century, so that they are between 130 and 200 years old. The largest and possibly the oldest oak, known as the Royal Oak, is located down near the lakeshore, where the river from O'Sullivan's Cascade enters the lake. Many of the oaks would have grown from seedlings during the Famine years (1845–49). Acorns are a source of food to many animals, and the more that are eaten the less chance there is of tree regeneration. At the birth of these oaks there had been a decline in the goat and deer population in the area (many were eaten during the Great Famine). Unlike other trees oak saplings are happier in open land, and do not tend to appear under tree canopies. However, there is concern amongst conservationists about the absence of young oak seedlings. These are essential to the regeneration of the oak forests.

WALK 18
THE GAP OF DUNLOE

LENGTH:	5.5 km.
DURATION:	2 to 2½ hours.
DIFFICULTY:	Along a paved road. Downhill then flat, followed by a gradual incline.
INTEREST:	Arguably the finest landscape in Ireland. A 'must do' for the visitor to Killarney. Peaceful walk beside lakes through a valley.
START/FINISH:	The car park opposite Kate Kearney's public house.
OPTIONS:	A jaunting car may be taken to the top of the walk, so that the walk back is then virtually all downhill. Kate Kearney's is a renowned Irish pub with good food and drink served. Walk over the Gap down into the Black Valley to Lord Brandon's Cottage and return to Killarney by boat.

Gap of Dunloe

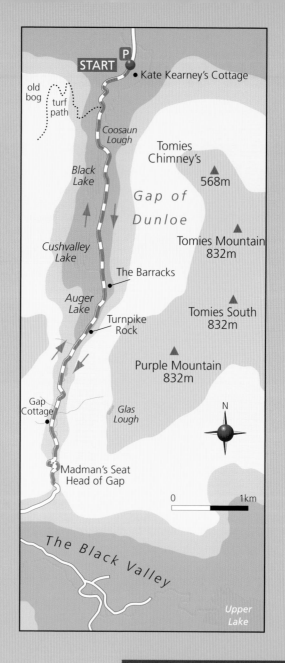

old bog

turf path

START

P

Kate Kearney's Cottage

Coosaun Lough

Tomies Chimney's 568m ▲

Black Lake

Gap of Dunloe

Cushvalley Lake

Tomies Mountain 832m ▲

The Barracks

Auger Lake

Tomies South 832m ▲

Turnpike Rock

Purple Mountain 832m ▲

Gap Cottage

Glas Lough

N

Madman's Seat Head of Gap

0   1km

The Black Valley

Upper Lake

Gap of Dunloe

Kate Kearney's is a popular hostelry in the Gap of Dunloe

Jarveys ferry tourists through the Gap of Dunloe

The natural beauty of the Gap of Dunloe is revered in song and the experience does not disappoint. Invariably there will be others on the same walk. In the height of summer, cars passing through the Gap are frowned upon because they are considered to interfere with the jaunting cars and walkers.

Start

Taking the N72 from Killarney towards Killorglin we pass the district of Fossa, and we take the signposted road to the left towards Glencar. Along this road we will come to a road junction with the Gap of Dunloe signposted to our left. We drive up to Kate Kearney's and park in the spacious car park opposite it. There is a public toilet in the corner of the car park.

Outward Journey

Passing by Kate Kearney's we walk into the Gap through the area where the jarveys vie for custom. Making our way through the tethered ponies and parked jaunting cars we can't help but experience the pungent smell. The road meanders through woodland and emerges onto flat land. On our right there is a cliff of solid rock close to the road that is used by mountaineers training in rock climbing. The more adventurous may be seen climbing the high cliffs above us. There is a path on our right that we can see going up the mountain. This is a 'turf path', used to bring down peat that was cut on the plateau above. The remains of turf cutting can still be seen on the plateau today.

High above us on our left are the mountains of Tomies and Purple. The sharp, pointed peaks in front of the first mountain are known as 'Tomies Chimneys'. One of the climbing routes up the mountains is through these chimneys.

We pass Coosaun Lake, then the Black Lake. Cushvally Lake is a little away from the road. The long lake that runs alongside the road is Auger Lake, but it is often referred to as 'Echo Lake'. Each jaunting car that passes the lake will stop and the jarvey will shout, his voice bouncing off the cliffs on either side. The ruined building alongside the road was formerly a police station and is known as 'The Barracks'. As we rise, the road kinks through an enormous boulder that is split in two. This is 'Turnpike Rock'. At the last of the zigzags in the road before the Head of the Gap is a rock outcrop protruding below the road wall. This is 'Madman's Seat'. It refers to a time when an unfortunate frequented the area, hurling abuse at passing travellers.

From the Head of the Gap we can see down into the Black Valley. There is an alternative route from the Black Valley to Killarney, out past the local church and youth hostel.

Return

During a former ice age a glacier burst through the Head of the Gap bringing down many boulders from the cliffs on either side. The glacier carved a track up through the Gap and left many grooves as it smoothed the rock on the floor of the valley.

Our journey back is mainly downhill until we rise up out of the valley at the end. Rhododendron has invaded the Gap and it can be seen on either side of the road. It is particularly worrying around the first ruined structure on our left, which was known as 'Gap Cottage.'

High above Gap Cottage there is a lake hidden from view: Lough Googh. Translated from the Gaelic it is 'the lake of the cuckoo'. The Gap of Dunloe is renowned as a popular habitat for cuckoos where they can be regularly heard in the early summer. As we approach the rise up to Kate Kearney's, the wooded copse on our right contains many tree species, but holly is dominant.

Kate Kearney was a woman who lived in the Gap and her claim to notoriety was that she sold very strong poteen.

Evicted From The Gap Of Dunloe

In his book *Peaks and Valleys* the writer Timmy Doyle gives a vivid account of how his family lived in the Gap of Dunloe and were evicted in the 1950s. They had to make a difficult journey along the route of this walk up through the Head of the Gap into the Black Valley. Timmy's father described the journey as *'four miles of torture, but the tourists love it'*. There was no surfaced road then and the old truck that transported them overheated going up the hill. An extract from the book is contained in this author's guide to *Carrauntoohil and the MacGillycuddy's Reeks*.

Walking Guides from The Collins Press

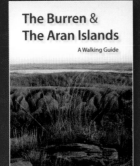

The Burren & The Aran Islands
A Walking Guide
Tony Kirby

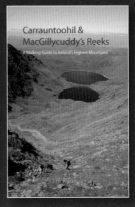

Carrauntoohil & MacGillycuddy's Reeks
A Walking Guide to Ireland's Highest Mountains
Jim Ryan

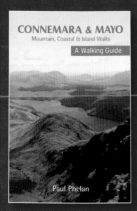

CONNEMARA & MAYO
Mountain, Coastal & Island Walks
A Walking Guide
Paul Phelan

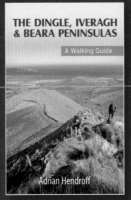

THE DINGLE, IVERAGH & BEARA PENINSULAS
A Walking Guide
Adrian Hendroff

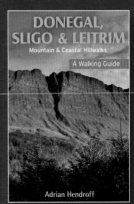

DONEGAL, SLIGO & LEITRIM
Mountain & Coastal Hillwalks
A Walking Guide
Adrian Hendroff

Walking Guides from
The Collins Press

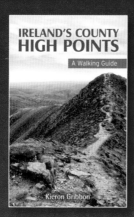

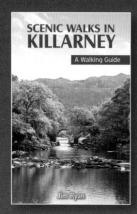

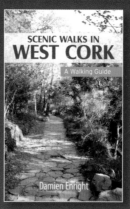

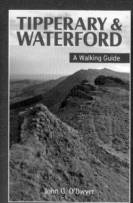